Weren' that bloke off the telly?

The joy of a life in journalism

To Steve and Wayne,

Enjoy!

Kevin

x

Kevin Burch

Front cover photograph by John Fairhall

ISBN 978-1-915292-72-8

Printed in Great Britain by
Biddles Books Limited, King's Lynn, Norfolk

Contents

Chapter One

Trust Me!

It was the moment when optimism and pessimism clashed head-on, as the lecturer looked out across the class of naive and wide-eyed trainee journalists and warned us, "Once you've finished this course, you'll never believe a single word you read."

Harsh, I thought at the time, but, forty-odd years on from that moment at Harlow Technical College in 1978, I realise, sadly, that the cynicism was well-placed and, more to the point, accurate and honest. Two words which would form the pillars of our working lives, as we learned quickly in the formative days ahead of the need, not just to chase the news, but to check and challenge, constantly to ensure that the Is and Ts on our clumsy, clattering, manual typewriters were dotted and crossed.

For reporters, especially with today's plethora of fake news, it's never been harder to separate the wheat from the chaff, and I've lost count of the number of stories - mostly red-top yarns - leads and tip-offs that I've been asked to follow up and which turned out to be completely without foundation, either in part, or in totality. Or the number of times at the scene of a story that I've been told by onlookers what's happened, only to see it contradicted over and over and discarded, promptly, as ill-informed speculation. Or read accounts elsewhere of the same stories I've covered, and been left wondering how that version of events could've strayed so far from what I saw and heard, and established as fact.

Yes, we all make mistakes; indeed, one of my favourite maxims has always been that he who never made a mistake never made anything. And in the maelstrom of today's news, when stories need to be delivered at breakneck speed, often in the form of what producers love to call "the rant" (essentially, just rattling off a whole stream of information in one unedited take), the pressure hits fever-pitch, as you screech to a halt and literally fall out of your car at the scene and try in milliseconds to work out what the hell has actually happened. Another favourite rule is - Never Assume Anything, else you could make an Ass out of U and Me.

Gossip, of course, is currency. "I promised I wouldn't say anything, but…" Bystanders aren't liars, but they do love to get involved, to feel involved - especially when they see a camera - and, when facts are either scarce or non-existent, the vacuum needs to be filled with something, invariably complete and utter tosh, so it pays to be on your guard from the off. It's the old rule of ABC: Assume nothing, Believe no one and Check everything. And, if you're not sure about it, don't run it.

> *"In the case of news, we should always wait for the sacrament of confirmation."*
>
> VOLTAIRE.

Another wise old sage at journalism college produced a golden rule which has remained with me, too, and it's about diligently checking people's names, so you get them right. And it's no good asking them, once they've told you, "And that's the normal spelling?" Of course it's normal, to them; they've lived with it since day one. I routinely get them to tell me, letter by letter and, even then, show them what I've written down. If you do fail on this one the viewer, or reader, can justifiably question the value of everything else you seek to lay before them.

Facts aren't negotiable. Facts are facts and, when you get them from the horse's mouth - someone who is at the very heart of the story - you realise that they are like gold dust; they are the Holy Grail we seek.

And it remains a source of huge pride that, during my career working in the Fourth Estate, I have never tried to manipulate the facts of a story; nor have I ever been asked to do so by an editor or producer. I have simply tried to tell it like it is. It's been heart-breaking at times; it's been a hoot, too. Never a dull moment.

Chapter Two

Scones to Scoops

I've always had a passion for food. It's probably the main reason why I was nicknamed Tubby at school! I remember one cookery lesson in which we made Eccles Cakes. There were six of them, big blighters, looking and smelling gorgeous, which I tucked into a plastic container. The problem was that I then had time on my hands and sat in the school library, trying to catch up on some studying, until the moment came to head home. But, by that time, the box was empty. My tummy was full. My mother would've been so proud of my culinary creations, if only she'd been given the chance to savour them!

So, given that the best advice when choosing a career seems to be to do something that you love, it was hardly a surprise that my instincts – or, rather, my nostrils - led me to the renowned kitchens at Ipswich Civic College, where I sought a place on a course in Hotel and Catering.

It seemed the perfect fit, until a member of the interview panel which would ultimately accept me into the college pointed out that the pay wasn't great, as most employees lived in, the hours were long, and I'd probably be working while everyone else was off and out enjoying themselves, and then off and out trying to enjoy myself while everyone else was working. I decided against it.

I looked at other options: a job with Lunn Poly in the travel business; again came a warning about low pay, offset by the odd free, foreign jaunt; the Civil Service, which seemed inherently slow and governed by rigid structures; and ICI, where, during the interview, in what now seems like a highly enlightened moment of foresight, my interviewer suggested I would be wasted in the particular role they had on offer and advised me to do something which was more suited to my outgoing, extrovert personality!

But, still undecided, it was back to the careers section of the school library, where someone equally smart - John Eaton, my geography and careers teacher - asked me if I'd ever thought about the media. Now, it has to be said that the media section I perused subsequently was small. The media weren't the sought-after, fashionable "mee-ja" destination they are today; and remember, too, this was in an educational setting where the focus was on university, especially Oxbridge. It wasn't hacks they wanted, but high-fliers. However, the booklet which I'd found spoke to me; quietly, but it spoke to me nonetheless. It was, I seem to recall, entitled something like - So You Want to be a Newsreader? Well, I'd always loved putting on a performance - usually in class during lessons, much to the frustration of my teachers, who noted this inability to focus consistently in their frequently unflattering comments in my school reports.

I also earned a reputation as a joker and prankster. The one of which I was most proud involved a group of us, who scuttled off to a classmate's house at lunchtime and recorded, on to an old reel-to-reel tape recorder, a little skit where we pretended that we were having a drinks party, clinking glasses, amid laughter and merriment, and wished our peers well in their A-level exams. I put my voice to it, and the most dangerous bit was when I hesitated over a word beginning with F, repeating the F several times - F-F-F-F-F-F - before finally coming out with it, leading to the obvious assumption to anyone listening that I was about to let fly with a profanity. We then, with the help of a few others, rigged up the tape machine under the stage in the school hall, left it ready to play, with the tape lined up with a length of carefully-calculated blank at the start so that, once switched on, it would have a spell of silence before the sound appeared, and then wired it up to the main speakers in the hall, plugged the machine, via an extension cable, into a socket in the hall, easily accessible just inside the door, and left, surreptitiously, the scene of the potential crime. We had worked out exactly when the switch on the socket needed to be thrown so that, a few minutes after the morning assembly began, the drinks party recording would magically appear.

Straws were drawn to see who'd handle the switch-on, and the lucky candidate, with us watching from a safe distance, went in and did the deed, returning with a clear smile of satisfaction. All set!

So, in we strode to assembly. No going back now, and I think we secretly doubted that the plan would work at all but, as the moment of truth drew near, with us no doubt studying our watches, suddenly a tell-tale, but relatively quiet "click" came from the speakers. We knew then that the tape was running and, sure enough, just seconds later, the performance began, much to the amusement of most of the pupils in the hall, but to the frustration of the teachers, some of whom dashed behind the curtains to find the source. The device, though, was well tucked away underneath the stage, so it kept playing; the damage was done. There followed a full inquest, as the suspected culprits were hauled in to see the deputy head, but the beauty of the plot was that a technically astute member of the gang strategically placed a magnet on the tape machine, so that, as the tape played and emerged through the heads, it passed the magnet and was promptly erased. Brilliant! No incriminating evidence. I think even some of the teaching staff were privately quite impressed by our ingenuity.

So, it was all high jinks and crazy capers for much of my latter school life but, thankfully, one of the teachers, Steve Wooldridge, who displayed remarkable insight and patience, had seen an alternative outlet for all this creative energy - the stage. School productions gave me that freedom to entertain. *HMS Pinafore* and Bertolt Brecht's superb *The Resistible Rise of Arturo Ui*, a parable play about a mobster trying to control the black-market trade in cauliflowers, with a satirical nod to the rise of Adolf Hitler and the Nazi Party in the lead-up to World War II.

It's a work - just like Alexander Solzhenitsyn's *One Day in the Life of Ivan Denisovich*, or Shakespeare's *Hamlet* - which I would only truly understand later in life. For this boy, at this moment in time, it was simply a chance to dress up in cool, 1930s clothes, wear make-up, perform and provoke a response from those around me - legitimately!

So, the idea of being centre-stage on screen, a journalist, telling the world what had happened, seemed just the ticket, although I had no idea of the nuts and bolts of the industry, nor how competitive it would be trying to get that door to creak slowly open. I applied to the local paper - the *East Anglian Daily Times* - seeking to be sponsored on a one-year Pre-Entry Journalism Course at Harlow. Lots of other people had the same idea, so the slots which were up for grabs were grabbed pretty quickly. But, undeterred, I tried a different route, and secured a local council grant to help pay for my studies. I was in, albeit with less money to spend on food and beer, but at least I was in. Was I ready? Was journalism ready? We were about to find out.

Chapter Three

Savouring Squiggles

Never mind about the challenges I'd face once in college, just getting there was a mission in itself. We travelled to Harlow early on Monday morning, stayed in digs with a local family, and then headed home again on Friday afternoon.

A fellow student, Will Bramhill, had a car, so he did the driving and picked me up at Brantham. That was where my dad worked, so I would take the family car first thing, leave it there and walk down the road to meet Will. Dad would then get a lift into work and drive the car home. The same thing happened in reverse on a Friday.

The journey itself seemed to take an age, not least because Will's car was, I recall, an old Austin/Morris 1300, and there were usually two other students on board as well as us two - Kevin Piper and Roger Ryan. The completion of the Monday trip was invariably marked by a loud rendition of Thin Lizzy's *The Boys Are Back in Town*, although I'm sure that Harlow probably had more important things to do than savour our arrival, after yet another epic trek along the A120.

The course itself was intense. A huge amount crammed into 12 months of study. Law, Public Administration, Use of English, Typing and Shorthand. Ah yes, shorthand. Forget everything else, this was what really mattered. This was what set apart the best from the rest. And that's why, for what felt like every moment of the day, we were staring at squiggles. Pitman New Era it was called. The wildest, weirdest shapes, which would allow us to jot down speeches and quotes at lightning speed and then, crucially, transcribe them, correctly, word for word. It wasn't just a case of memorising the shapes, but realising that where they were placed - above the line; through the line; under the line - and what dots and dashes went with them, would be crucial in navigating the nuances and subtleties of this most bizarre but beautiful new way of writing.

We were blessed to have a tutor who was always immaculately dressed, caring and funny, but boy, did she drive us on relentlessly. The text got more complex, the speeds got faster and all the time you knew that, once you lost the pace, you were lost completely. Trying to memorise what had been said in that instant, and still have an ear absorbing the next bit, was the stuff of nightmares.

I wasn't the smartest scholar, but I did work out pretty quickly that a high shorthand speed was the passport to success, and so, in my digs in Potter Street in Harlow, up in my room, most nights were spent going over and over those squiggles time and time again. It was, in hindsight, an advantage that I had little money from my grant to spend on socialising, although we did all venture out most Thursday evenings to a club in Old Harlow, which used to host some amazing live bands. Too much time away from my bedroom and my desk would've been a distraction I didn't need.

Typing, too - at real speed - was a skill we also had to master. Smashing the keys with just two fingers at first, but gradually and gently learning to use all of them, eyes forward, not down, and knowing instinctively, from memory, where every individual letter, number and symbol could be found – caressing, not clouting the machine. And, again, the end result had to be 100% accurate and neat.

Gradually the typing speed increased, until I hit the dizzy heights of forty words per minute in test conditions, against the stopwatch.

As for my shorthand, well that, too, got faster and faster. It was all-consuming. So much so that, as the students' review show at the end of the year drew near, we had to think of a fitting format and, from me, what else but a song I wrote and performed with others especially for the occasion about, *The Shorthand Blues*.

But, as the course headed to a conclusion, the most important thing was finding a job. Some of the sponsored students had theirs already lined up but for me, well, it was back to the *East Anglian Daily Times*, and a meeting with the paper's then Editor, Don Simpson, who gave me a target to hit. Secure an exam grade of 120 words per minute shorthand,

and there's an opening. Suddenly, all those seemingly endless long nights of study, all that re-tracing of outlines with fingers in mid-air - no matter where I was - and all those sweat-inducing sprints against the stopwatch in class, made perfect sense. And, come the moment which mattered, that target of 120 words per minute was in the bag… and I was in work, taken on as a "junior journalist". Love that. I still have a copy of my "Articles of Apprenticeship and Employment", dated 23rd July 1979. It would cover a period of two years and three months, during which time the company would "to the best of its power, skill and knowledge, instruct the junior journalist in the profession of journalist and in all things appertaining thereto." This was it. Next stop, north Suffolk, and the district office in Halesworth. In what proved a pivotal weekend, my brother Terry got married on the Saturday and, on the Sunday - 22nd July 1979 - Mum, Dad and I loaded up all my worldly goods onto a small, flat-back lorry, watched over anxiously by Jet, our pet dog at the time, and then we sallied forth, up the A12 to a delightful market town of which I'd never heard. My accommodation for the duration would be a huge flat, situated at one end of the main Thoroughfare. It was right next door to the chippie. Marvellous. Hello to a new home. All hail the new hack!

Journalism can never be silent: that is its greatest value. It must speak, and speak immediately, while the echoes of wonder, the claims of triumph, and the signs of horror are still in the air."

HENRY ANATOLE GRUNWALD

Chapter Four

Hello, is That *The Sun?*

New hack, old technology!

First things first. Don't be fooled into trying to clean that mark off the picture - it's on the original! And yes, that's what we used to call a phone, and that's a manual typewriter. A portable one, by the look of it. The other machine in the rear office at Halesworth was a hefty beast. I think it was an *Olympia* model, and we always used to take a carbon copy of everything we wrote. The copy went on a spike, while the original went off in an envelope with the rest of the day's output by train to Head Office in Ipswich. If you missed it, everything had to be dictated by phone although, some years later, we did savour the arrival of modem kits, with rubber suckers which sat over the earpiece and mouthpiece, and it was a mysterious, almost sci-fi-like sound which did the rest - sometimes! Sometimes it would get lost in translation. Anyway, I digress, because this office would be home for the initial few years of my newspaper career.

To start with I was given the onerous task of writing-up wedding reports for the weekly paper, *The Halesworth Times and Southwold Mercury*, where the bride almost always had Lily of the Valley in her bouquet and was invariably given away by her father. Repetitive, undoubtedly, but the expectation was that each account would be written with care and, whenever possible, with flair. If the original family notes told you that the bride arrived on an old fire engine, the urge to use a line like, *Love Me Tender* would be irresistible. If the vehicle broke down on the way to church, so much the better. It all added to the colour. It was often tedious but, essentially, it was a discipline which mattered, and which required an eye for detail. Why? Because get a simple thing wrong and the readers knew where to find you. There was no hiding place in a prominent district office, sitting on the main Thoroughfare.

But knowing where to find you paid dividends, too, when people had a story to tell. You were, invariably, their obvious first port of call. Also, there were monthly town and parish council meetings, which had to be covered and sometimes had to be seen to be believed, as the progress through the agenda repeatedly stalled, and the discussions stretched late into the night, often over things like whether the grass on the town greens in Southwold had been cut to the correct height. If not, a letter would be despatched with haste, and with words of castigation, to those responsible.

But suddenly, in the midst of it all, would come that headline-creating moment of brilliance. A councillor thumping the table in a fury, using words like "shameful" and "disgrace", insisting someone be held to account - the local MP called in to take up the cudgels.

One issue I remember well was the threat to close local schools, through reorganisation. It was one which provoked local fury and would eventually lead to a huge protest march on the old county council building in St Helen's Street in Ipswich, where banners would be waved, slogans shouted - normally including the words "What do we want... ?" - in a drive to prevent the axe falling. Journalists always love the metaphor of an axe falling, even if the imagery of it falling onto a school building makes no sense at all!

Anyway, back to the council meetings. They were, of course, local democracy in action - in full flow – and, invariably, the councillors would glance towards the press table just before they let rip, to ensure that the reporter's pen was suitably poised and also, no doubt, to ensure he or she hadn't nodded off.

Invariably, you'd be on your own, which meant you would truly be first with the news and, if more than one little nugget popped up, which was often the case, you could run with one and save another for another day - a rainy day. None of this journalism/"churnalism" of today. This was as fresh as it got.

I mentioned "no hiding place" earlier, and it wasn't just the readers who knew where to find you. My chief reporter in those early days was always on the case, too, suggesting a string of possible stories and regularly popping her head round the door to check how things were going.

One day I remember well. The story was about a woman who lived in Holton Road - a short walk from the office - and had been complaining about sewage seeping from a manhole and pooling across her garden. I went along, not entirely enamoured of the tale, so I either knocked very lamely on the door, or didn't even do that; I can't recall exactly how much energy I expended on what was a pretty simple task.

Anyway, I scooted back to the office, claiming that the owner had been nowhere to be seen.

Sure enough, a few minutes later, the phone rang in the chief's office, and the snippets of conversation - "Oh, didn't he?", "I'm so sorry, he told me he knocked on the door," "I can only apologise" - told me all I needed to know. Rumbled? You bet! In she came, feeling, quite rightly, badly let down by this young cub reporter, who'd lied through his teeth. It was the one and only time that I baulked. Lesson learned.

Someone who also knew where to find me was a local councillor I knew well, who called me one night to suggest I might want to pop round to his house the next day, with a photographer, as he had a story.

We arrived to find out that his wife had taken an egg, which had been rejected by one of their hens, and went to bed that night, wearing her bra, with this egg nestled in the cleavage. She must've had a hunch that there was a chick inside and, sure enough, in the morning, it hatched, and she called it Bluey! We got a lovely pic of the chick with her, nestling in the, it has to be said, capacious bra.

Well, after I'd sorted the story for the paper, I called *The Sun* and told the news desk about Bluey. Needless to say, they loved it, and paid for it. Next day, the headline - on page 3, I recall - was something like, "You Lucky Chick"!

But there was more! The councillor called me within hours to tell me that Bluey had been too weak, and didn't last long. We did the story and, again, I called *The Sun*, thinking that, this time, they might dismiss it; but no, they loved it, and paid for more copy, and even sent the family some flowers with an RIP note - from *The Sun* and its readers! Nice touch.

Chapter Five

Keep Digging

One of the key qualities in journalism is tenacity. It always makes me smile when people say that the media will get bored and leave things alone. They might if it's a busy day, but they probably won't. It's what they're trained and paid to do. And nothing piqued my interest more than someone suggesting, "There's nothing to see here, move on."

One story, which remains one of the most tragic I've covered, came to light initially only because of the determination of someone else, who realised that certain things didn't add up.

She was one of the newspaper's invaluable village correspondents, who'd feed us snippets of parish-pump copy and who we'd sometimes meet for a coffee to catch up on local chit-chat.

She called me one day to say that some residents had been talking about a woman who hadn't been seen in town for some time. It was all very baffling. No one could work out what had happened. If I'm honest, I let it go, in the belief that it was something which would be resolved eventually and, probably, innocently.

But the correspondent wouldn't let it go and, every time we spoke over the next few weeks, it was the one thing about which she kept reminding me. There was washing left on the line at the house where she lived, but no sign of the lady. There was someone inside though, she went on to tell me, who'd been seen to pass money through an open window, to pay for things like a milk delivery.

We often had days when the normally frenetic pace of news eased and things were quiet; days when we'd be encouraged to hit the road and seek out what were called off-diary stories. So, this was the chance to do some digging, and it didn't take long to uncover the tragic truth about what had happened. I knew the address but, after getting no response at the house, which seemed deserted, I knocked on the door of the neighbours. I told them that I was from the local paper, looking into what might have happened next door, and they kindly invited me in and told me, over a pot of tea, everything they knew.

The house was home to a mother and daughter. The mother, who was 90 years old, had passed away and it seemed that, unable to accept the fact that she'd died, the daughter, who was devoted to her, left her in bed, taking her cups of tea, talking to her, and shut herself away from the outside world. The home was spotless. For how long this had been going, at this stage, the neighbours could only guess. They had, though, been worried for months. The only washing which appeared on the line was the daughter's, not the mother's. She refused offers of help but, eventually, they called in social services. The police finally gained entry and found the body. It was just days before Christmas, 1984. It was so desperately sad.

Once back in the office, I put in a call to the police, and ended up speaking to a senior detective, who had always been really open and honest with me in the past, but told me that, on this one, there was really nothing he could tell me apart from the fact that they'd investigated the case and there was nothing suspicious. The coroner had been informed.

I called the newsroom in Ipswich to let them know what we had, and wrote up the story. It ran under the headline: Daughter's Tragic Secret of Dead Mother Upstairs.

A few weeks later came the inquest, which was held at Lowestoft Police Station.

During the hearing came confirmation of everything we'd been told.

Reassuring as it was to know that I'd got the story and, more importantly, got it right, what struck me most then - and still to this day - is the heartbreaking nature of what happened. A daughter who couldn't face the possibility of being parted from the mother she adored. According to the evidence, she'd just blanked everything out, unable to comprehend what was happening. Harrowing.

Chapter Six

Lion Loose? Er, No!

Today, the relationship between the police and media is extremely well-choreographed and controlled. Everything, invariably, comes via the press office, as and when they're ready to release it, and not before. Tip-offs still come, but they're a rarity and, given the tight control within most forces, the prospect now of securing a nugget over a pint is virtually non-existent. Indeed, the whole notion of either the press or the police actually being in the pub, engaged in cosy conversation, vanished long ago. You can sometimes still expect helpful guidance, along the lines of, "Would I look silly if I said this?" but, by and large, the official line will always take time to emerge because, quite simply and understandably, the police have to ensure their ducks are all in a row and, in so many cases, need to protect the integrity of a case. Prejudice is a word that rings alarm bells in both camps!

There was, though, a time when there was a simplicity and, perhaps, a naivety about how we got access to information. It was my job as a young reporter to trot up to the police station in Halesworth, with two copies of that morning's paper tucked under my arm. Once you'd handed them over to the civilian member of staff on the front desk, you'd be guided through the book which detailed all the activity of the past 24 hours and which, potentially, would make a line or two. Sometimes, if they were busy, the book would be turned around so you could go through it yourself, noting entries which had been marked-up for "no publicity". You knew not to push things, because this was a relationship built on trust. To betray it would cost you access to tiny titbits.

But one day, when I'd been left to my own devices, one entry instantly caught my eye - a circus vehicle which had overturned on the A12 at

Blythburgh, leading to a number of animals, including a lion, getting loose, but which, thankfully, the report said, had been rounded-up with the help of locals. Gold-dust!

I scuttled off back to the office (no mobiles then!) and started putting in calls to people I knew in that area, but no one seemed to know anything about it. It had, though, I reassured myself, come from the police, so I filed it across to Ipswich to meet the early deadline for the evening paper. In a millisecond, not surprisingly, the news desk was on the phone wanting more, so I called the police to see if we could get more information, only to discover that the entry in the log about the circus animals had been a test message only, and was clearly marked as such. I hadn't seen it. No wonder details were scarce. Imagine the ignominy, having to call the news desk back and explain that this breaking story hadn't broken at all! Not my finest moment, but a lesson learned. He who never made a mistake and all that! I have tried, in vain, while researching this book to find a cutting from that day. Strangely, it doesn't appear to exist but, believe me, it happened. Trust me - I'm a journalist, after all!

Chapter Seven

The Subs' Bench

Life in the district had become a very comfortable existence. Perhaps too comfortable. And when I look back through some of the old cuttings of stories I was doing at the time, maybe it's hardly surprising. "Minister rejects chance to view traffic congestion," "Protesting fisherman tells of cod quota struggle," (that was 1987, some things never change!), "Transform Southwold harbour plan attacked." And there was always dog mess! Nothing seemed to enrage people more. Take this Burchy classic, under the headline "Anti-dog campaign fouled up!" and, if I set out the first few lines, you'll get the gist:

"Footpath-fouling dogs in Southwold are getting away with their dirty tricks!

"The town's dirty dogs have given the slip to officers of Waveney District Council, who spent a week in the town in April in an effort to catch would-be four-legged offenders in the act, but without success.

"Two council officers patrolled the town every day during the week in the early morning, afternoon and night, but no offenders were caught during their total 60-hour surveillance."

And how about this one to make you feel old?

Under the headline, "Call for second 'phone box", it read:

"Reydon Parish Council finance and general purposes committee on Tuesday agreed to look into the possibility of having another telephone kiosk installed in the village."

Yes, phone kiosks. Most have today either been put to alternative uses, like mini-libraries, or vandalised beyond repair. In my early reporting days, pre-mobiles, the kiosk, with its inevitable scent of urine, damp phone directory or yellow pages with most of the pages missing, with its pips, with its option of a reverse-charge call if you'd scrabbled for spare cash and failed, was absolutely essential.

But as a story goes, I admit, that tale, that opening line would induce slumber.

And you can add to the list, "Super-style sunflowers" (growing tall ones contest), "Cat's capers" (feline runaway), "Road blocked", (er, road blocked), "Success for garage mechanic", (in the running for national grease-monkey title), "Scrump danger" (dodgy apples) and "Their brains left at home" (tourists parking on village greens shocker).

Some days, you'd end up smacking your head against the typewriter in frustration, as you struggled to compose that clever opening line to a story, especially when the content itself was less than inspiring. At the time, I used to smoke roll-up cigarettes while I was working, and preparing one of those bad boys was, I always maintained, a surefire way to get the journalistic juices going. But, when even the deep intake of nicotine failed to get the creative cogs whirring, I knew I was in trouble. It's worth saying that smoking in the office was something you were allowed to do then. In fact, my chief reporter at the time smoked like a chimney and setting foot in her office involved braving a thick smog which, on some days, seemed impenetrable. You'd come out kippered anyway, so it seemed sensible to create my own mini-cloud of pollution.

Outside of work, though, there was plenty to keep me amused. I had myself a lovely little Sunbeam Alpine convertible, in which I used to get around. It had the most amazing roar, especially when you scooted through the tight and echoing confines of the main Thoroughfare through town.

I'd also discovered a passion for snooker, along with my fellow reporter and flatmate Bill Izzard, which meant regular trips to the social club in Halesworth, where they had two full-sized tables upstairs. It became a haunt, not just in the evening but, increasingly, at lunchtime too, when the Gods of News allowed a lull in the proceedings. The office always knew the number to ring and that call-to-arms would be relayed swiftly, with a yell up the stairs, by the steward behind the bar. Even if you were mid-frame, building a handsome score, or on the cusp of victory, we knew it was wise not to swing the lead. Play was halted,

19

The all-consuming Alpine.

cues placed back in the rack, and we were away, to who knew what? That was half the fun! The thrill of the chase. And, to be fair, there was no let-up in the flow of news. That tactic I mentioned earlier, of tucking a story or two in your back pocket for a rainy day, was working well. There was always plenty to keep headquarters happy and the pages filled.

But how, precisely, the next step on the ladder was decided, I can't recall. Probably the result of one of those lunches in the pub, with the news editor, setting out "objectives"! The feeling, I think, was that it might be wise to pull me out of the sticks for a while and return me to some form of civilisation at the heart of things. That meant the *East Anglian Daily Times*' head office building in Lower Brook Street in Ipswich, and my exact destination within that expansive warren of offices was the subs' room for the *Evening Star*.

It's worth pointing out that, in those days, this wasn't some high-tech, sterile setting. This was a place which lived and breathed. Where typewriters clattered; where the paper was actually printed; where you could feel the structure rumble when the presses were rolling; and where the team could still decide to "Hold the Front Page" if the big story broke late on. It was a place awash with real, larger-than-life characters, who knew how to have a laugh; who knew how to wind people up relentlessly; but, most of all, who knew their trade.

It was a time when unions had muscle and where jobs were clearly defined. You didn't walk out onto the seemingly cavernous space where the compositors worked and start picking things up. That was a definite no-no. Strict rules about who did what; who touched what. And it was an intimidating environment. The sight of a young journo strolling through would usually prompt a whistled, mocking tune. I remember once a near-miss, as a half-eaten cheese sandwich came twirling through the air in my direction. It would surely be frowned upon now but, then, it was banter - part of the learning process. In reality, these were people who cared, who watched your back, who'd be in the social club on a Friday, together with a pint, a reminder that we were all in this together. Part of one big family.

The sub's role was pivotal. To take the typed copy from the newsroom, which would be dished out by Carol Carver, the chief sub, at the head of the table, which was graded from top to bottom: the experienced hands sat close to the chief sub's shoulder and looked after the serious stuff - the front page, and the main ones which followed. New arrivals like me sat way down the other end, given the less critical bits and pieces, which meant we had more time to make progress - and make mistakes.

Once copy was processed, you had to open the hatch in the far end of the room and place the paper under a weight, to ensure the draught which whistled through didn't whip it away in a flash.

It was the sub's job to mark up the copy with instructions for the point size the text needed, to ensure that it would all fit into the space you'd been allocated in a given column, on a given page. The main body of the piece was pretty standard, but the fun came in sorting out the headlines and subheads, which clearly needed to be chunkier to stand out - 36 point, or similar. We were trained to work out pretty accurately how much space a headline would need, based on the letters used and depending on the point size. A "W" or an "M" ate up more space than, say, an "I". Sometimes it fitted like a dream, sometimes you got your sums completely wrong. How we'd dread a comp appearing at the door, normally tapping a rule in his hand, to announce that they had "a buster". He'd reveal the page which was involved with great gusto and, if it was yours, you'd have to head out onto the floor and help work out if a word could be taken out, to make it fit, while still allowing it to make sense, or whether the whole thing had to be done again. The clock was always ticking.

Headlines could be a curse, but some days you could be struck by moments of pure brilliance.

I remember one story about a restaurant which had been plunged into chaos when someone nicked the diary containing all their reservations. The headline I thought up? "Guess Who's Coming to Dinner?" And, for the story about a worker retiring from a career in revenue and customs, I managed something about finally being duty-free!

I mentioned earlier about feeling the presses rolling, and there was never a sweeter moment than when a swathe of the first and freshly-printed copies arrived in the room, normally draped over someone's arm, and you could savour the beauty of what you'd created, with the ink hardly dry!

It was also one of the funniest spells in my time at the paper. Even though I'd swapped my convertible for a motorbike - a Honda 125 - and travelled in to work every day from Halesworth, no matter what the weather, and frequently arrived soaked to the skin, I loved every moment. Halcyon days, always filled with laughter.

Chapter Eight

Seal of Approval

I spent a year as a sub. It was just the most joyous time, working with a bunch of people who took their work seriously, but never themselves! They were wise, witty and wondrously funny. We had nicknames, too. Mine was Hardwick. Goodness knows where that came from, but it was a moniker which stuck, and still does today whenever I cross paths with one particular fellow ex-sub.

I did have one other role during that time, and that was writing a column for the *Star*, where we'd review something which had been on the box last night. It was called Teleview.

Writing had always been a passion. I can remember my parents hauling me away from the visitor's book, when we spent time away anywhere. The hosts, I suspect, really only expected a line or two. I'd been intent on giving them a novel.

So, this was a chance to wax lyrical, at a time when I was mostly sorting other people's written work, and not creating my own.

I still have some of the old Teleview cuttings. There was one I wrote about Rik Mayall's debut as the dodgy MP Alan Beresford B'Stard in ITV's *The New Statesman*, noting how the phrase "fluffy bottom" got the best laugh of the night, and another piece reflected on a programme about euthanasia, with me drawing comparisons over how a family handles the loss of a pet dog, and concluding:

"An unfair comparison maybe, but personally I hope that when my nose dries up and my coat loses its shine, someone will have the compassion to afford me a painless and dignified end."

That one was published on 25th September, 1987. My stance in that particular debate hasn't shifted.

The column, too, was a reminder of something which I would realise many times in my journalistic career, and that is - you never know who's out there, reading, listening, or watching.

I wrote a pretty simple piece about a boxing contest featuring two giants of the ring, Frank Bruno and Joe Bugner, but it was broadcast on ITV, not the BBC, so the legend that was Harry Carpenter wasn't at ringside doing the commentary on Frank's big night. I noted how sad it was not to be able to savour the wonderful bond between the pair, and Bruno's inevitable post-fight catchphrase, "Know what I mean 'arry?"!

A few days later, out of the blue, a letter arrived at the *Star*'s offices and, when I opened it, it was from Harry Carpenter himself, who'd written on 17th November, 1987 how "a lady from Ipswich has sent

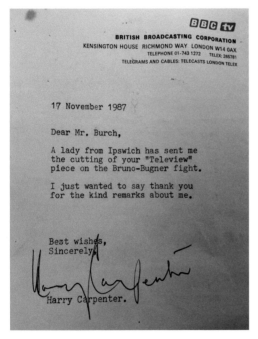

me the cutting of your 'Teleview' piece on the Bruno-Bugner fight. I just wanted to say thank you for the kind remarks about me." He added his best wishes and signed it.

How fabulous was that? How wonderful that he took the trouble? Just five lines, but it meant the world, not least because it was written on BBC TV-branded paper! The fact I still have it today tells you everything.

Another piece which struck a chord was about snooker, and my observations that sometimes the TV commentators just needed to shut up!

I wrote it in April 1985, and it clearly chimed with the cartoonist Carl Giles, who lived on the outskirts of Ipswich at the time, as he sent me subsequently a signed copy of a picture he'd produced, which depicted Grandma Giles lobbing objects at the telly, with the caption,

"She's still in an uncontrollable rage over the babbling BBC commentators for ruining her snooker tournament"!

" She's still in an uncontrollable rage over the babbling BBC commentators for ruining her snooker tournament "

To Kevin Busch —
Best wishes,
from Giles

Hillbrow Farm
Witnesham
Suffolk
IP6 9HL

April 16th '85

Dear Kevin Busch,

Your splendid piece today— I thought I was the only one who felt like that about the morons.

Many thanks!
Carl Giles

With it came a handwritten note from Giles praising what he thought was a "splendid piece", adding, "I thought I was the only one who felt like that about the morons."

Hardly surprising that it's a gift I've cherished ever since, and it hangs proudly on a wall at home.

The *Evening Star* savoured it too, running the story on

the front page, with the headline, "The Star is right on cue for Giles!" Nice.

What struck me most, in both cases, was that two important people who, no doubt, had a huge number of very important things to do, had taken the trouble to make contact in such a generous, kind-spirited way.

And it was something I was to see time and again when in the presence of celebrity figures.

I remember another "off-diary" day, when I went in search of a story and ended up in Southwold. This often involved looking at noticeboards and stickers in shop windows, as well as popping your head into High Street shops, or calling at the council offices, or visiting regular contacts who had their finger on the pulse.

But when all that failed, I went strolling down towards the sea, past Adnams brewery and the lighthouse at East Green and, as I drew closer to the beach, I heard music drifting in my direction, over the rows of brightly-coloured beach huts, on the stiff, onshore breeze.

It was actually the sound of the Southwold & Reydon Corps of Drums, and they were marching along the prom and being filmed. Now I had always had a keen eye for a famous face, and I was pretty sure that the chap who was sitting by the pier, deep in thought, was Michael Palin. I knew him, of course, from Monty Python, but this was, I think, 1986, so it was before he became better known as a globe-trotting TV presenter.

Convinced it was him and with curiosity aroused, I waited until the filming was halted and he rose to his feet, and walked up to him, opening with the obvious line, "Excuse me, it's Michael Palin, isn't it?" It turned out that this was a TV drama in the making, *East of Ipswich*, to be precise, which was loosely based on Palin's own childhood memories of seaside holidays in the 1950s.

Now I might've been young, but I wasn't stupid. I could see that Palin was busy, so I asked whether, if I returned later with a photographer, he would spare some time to tell me more about the filming and allow us to take a few pictures. He could, of course, have told me that he was way too busy to pause during what I suspect was a hectic production schedule to indulge a young reporter from the local paper, but he didn't.

In fact, he couldn't have been kinder and we duly met later, by the pier, and he gave me chapter and verse.

The film itself went out on the BBC the following year, 1987, and was described by Palin as "the happiest and least complicated creative project" in which he'd ever been involved. Maybe that was it. Happy, relaxed and working on something about which he clearly felt hugely passionate. Perhaps that was why he was more than keen to share the story of what was taking shape that day on the front. Whatever the reason, it was the classic demonstration of that line that "it's nice to be important, but it's more important to be nice." Palin was the epitome of charm, and I never forgot it.

Another famous face was the jazz-drummer, bandleader and TV musical director, Jack Parnell, who'd retired to Southwold in 1983, I suspect, for a quiet life. He was a keen golfer, and word reached me that he was in the patch, so I found out where he was living and knocked on the door. He answered, which kind of took the wind out of my sails, because I simply hadn't expected it. Again, he explained that it wasn't convenient just then, but we fixed a date for a meeting, at which we talked at length about his life and our photographer captured a beautiful shot of Jack sitting at his grand piano in the front room. He was a giant in the world of music, and a gent. Parnell kept on playing for pleasure well into his eighties. He had his own quartet, which would perform regularly in a couple of local pubs. It was in Southwold that he died in 2010. He was 87.

Chapter Nine

Radio Calling

I'd had a stint as a sub, and I'd then returned to the districts. For the simple reason that I loved being there. It gave me a sense of freedom and the ability to get as close to real people and real stories as you could. Some of the major ones remain, vividly, in the mind. The disastrous fire in 1984 at the majestic Grade-Two-Listed Heveningham Hall was one.

I was living on London Road in Halesworth at the time, and can remember the local fire crew heading out of town, sirens on. In no time at all, another followed in its wake. The only thing to do was jump in the car and go too, heading out on the Walpole Road. But even before I'd reached the hall itself, I could see the amber glow in the sky, and the repetitive sweep of blue from the emergency vehicles who'd already arrived, in numbers.

Minutes later, I was there too, looking out in disbelief across the lake to my left, as the flames ripped through the roof of the East Wing. The building was undergoing restoration at the time, having been sold by the Government in 1981 to an Iraqi businessman, Abdul Amir Al-Ghazzi, who guarded his privacy zealously. The damage caused was well in excess of £3 million.

It became a running story of real significance. Pressure building to get the 18th-century mansion repaired and restored to its former glory. It would prove convoluted and complex.

The one thing, though, which was always guaranteed, was variety, as revealed by a flick through some of the cuttings I kept.

There were remarkable stories of survival. Like the microlight pilot who - in that same year - hit an 11,000-volt power cable at Bramfield and crashed to the ground. Both he and his co-pilot lay trapped for

20 minutes in the wreckage, which was entangled in the wires and, effectively, live. I remember his description of the pair sparking every time they moved, and admission that they were lucky to be alive.

And stories of sheer fascination. A feature on the Victorian brickworks at South Cove, producing 12,000 a week, using, at the time, the oldest kiln of its type still in commercial use. Or officials trying to decide what to do with the rotting carcass of a huge Minke whale washed up on the beach, or the attempt to blow apart an old wartime concrete bunker from the sandy cliffs just north of Easton Bavents, because it was deemed a danger. The cliffs gave way; the bunker didn't. It ended up on the beach below, still remarkably intact!

And there were, of course, events like the great storm of 1987. I was living in a cottage at Badingham at the time and, all around, there seemed utter chaos after the ferocious overnight winds had carved their way through the county, bringing down trees and buildings. Countless stories to tell, but I was about as much use as a chocolate teapot. No way out and no way in. We were stranded in the village. Like so many others, completely isolated from the outside world.

I can remember, once a few routes had been cleared, making it to Cransford, just a short way down the road, where the wall of the local Methodist chapel had been flattened.

And every time since, that I've been called by the news desk to be told that such-and-such is cut off by snow, floods, whatever, and asked if I could head there and see what I could get, I remember that moment and smile!

But these were the highlights. The truth was that life on the paper was starting to feel a bit like *Groundhog Day*, and I knew I needed something fresh.

Like most people, I listened to the radio in the car, but I knew nothing about the mechanics of what went on behind the scenes.

Then, a chance too good to miss. A job advert for a News Producer at BBC Radio Norfolk in Norwich. A news producer, presumably producing just news. That didn't sound too hard.

I went for the interview but, critically, I did very little homework. So, when we got down to the detail, like knowing what a "cart" machine is, I was floundering. I resisted the temptation to be funny, and suggest something agricultural but, needless to say, I didn't get the job. (Cart, as anyone with an ounce of radio knowledge knows, was a cartridge, i.e., the bit of kit onto which a news piece was recorded and which could then be thrust into the machine to play out, when the right button was hit, or fader opened). But I did get a helping hand from someone on the interview board, David Line, who suggested that I should come in one weekend to see what actually went on, as they felt that, with my journalistic experience, I had plenty to offer.

So I did. It was just captivating, and the most exciting thing? Not just one deadline a day, but a deadline every hour, without fail. I was blessed to be mentored by Ian Hyams, someone with heaps of experience. Unflappable, calm and incredibly trusting. So, when he asked if I'd like to read the next bulletin I, of course, said yes, and that was it. Minutes later, I was behind the mic being introduced and rattling my way through the scripts, and firing off the carts. It all went smoothly and everyone seemed impressed and, fortunately for me, when the next news producer job came up, I applied and was in. The official letter came soon after, confirming that my employment would start on 3rd May 1988. I cannot tell you how proud I was to know that I'd be working for the BBC. It was a slight step down in money, but a step up, I had no doubt, in my career. I let the *East Anglian* know that I'd be off and, with all the paperwork complete, that was that.

My first day at work at Norfolk Tower was, however, slightly bizarre. As a paid-up member of the NUJ, it just so happened that on that pivotal morning we were to form a picket line outside the building, in protest at the BBC's plans to make a 10% cut across the corporation. Hardly ideal, but I think the station manager, Keith Salmon, was nonetheless pleased to see me, even though I had effectively downed tools on day one!

Eventually, I got to work, but, bizarrely, this didn't feel like work at all. It felt the most natural thing in the world to be in the radio newsroom, writing what was a much more condensed form of words. No time to get all flowery, like newspaper copy. This had to be sharp and to the point, and the deadlines kept coming, so everything had to be freshened up every hour. We gathered local news, which we gleaned from either morning check-calls to the emergency services, or our own rolling diary and the papers, and we mixed it with national audio and copy, which came to us on a feed from London called GNS, *General News Service*. There were clips (soundbites of people talking), voice-pieces (reporters talking) or wraps (a reporter making a sandwich with their words, either side of a quick burst of someone else talking).

These were terrific, if somewhat tiring days. I was still living in Suffolk, so left home at about 4am if I was covering the early shift, and drove to Norwich, returning home in the afternoon and, especially on blissfully warm summer days, struggling to stay awake.

But I was clearly doing something right, because a slot opened up to step in as Acting News Editor, to cover behind others who were going off on attachment, for a stint working elsewhere in the BBC. It meant chairing the morning news meeting, stimulating ideas, keeping everyone happy and invigorated and, above all else, making sure that what we were putting out wasn't just up-to-the-minute, but up to the mark in terms of BBC policy and the obvious legal constraints around contempt and libel. There was a huge amount to consider and often a minimal amount of time in which to do the thinking, but I think I displayed a wise head, and was blessed with a strong and supportive team around me.

It could be fast and furious but, boy, was it fun, too. Playing cricket down the length of the newsroom, or getting hauled in by presenters, like the irresistibly funny Roy Waller, to create characters on air. Mine was Cecil, the hapless fool, who'd always wander noisily into the studio at the wrong time, and invariably lean across the desk and hit the wrong button. I can remember taking part in a skit once where, with the clever use of sound effects, Roy was pretending to be roaring around in circles in the studio on a motorcycle. It was madcap and marvellous. We also devised a series of silly *Tannoy* announcements. "Sadly, this afternoon's course on self-motivation has been cancelled. The organiser couldn't be bothered to turn up," or, "The session on how to improve your driving will be delayed - the chap running it has just collided with the Radio Car." And it was then that I learned the magic rule of radio - that you never destroy the illusion. If a presenter tells his listeners that he's got a giraffe on a lead in the studio and he's trying to feed it carrots, then that's exactly what's going on. Play along. On another occasion, when Roy was due to be off on holiday, we pretended that I'd locked him in the loo and wouldn't let him out, so that I could present his show instead. It worked a treat, although I'm not sure his loyal listeners were too impressed with the stand-in!

I was incredibly happy though, as you can probably tell, and I was still commuting every day to Norwich. I'd thought about it, but hadn't yet managed to move house. However, it was probably good in the long run that I hadn't, because a new radio station would soon be taking to air, to serve the county of Suffolk. It was one of the few parts of the country which didn't have its own BBC local radio station. I was Suffolk born and bred and, while I knew they'd almost certainly be looking for a News Editor, I hadn't thought seriously about applying.

But then fate lent a hand. The man who would subsequently prove such a role model, mentor and inspiration in my career, Ivan Howlett, just happened to be visiting the station. At that stage I didn't really know much about him but, as I was walking back to the newsroom, I saw him approaching. He was chatting with Keith Salmon. We'd just passed each other and then he turned and said, "You are putting in for the job, aren't you?" What else was I meant to say but yes?! So I did.

Soon enough came the interview for the job. I'd done plenty of homework this time and, of course, I had a huge advantage. This was my patch. I knew my way around. Knew the people and places. I can't remember much about the questioning that day, but I do remember the panel were clearly looking for reassurance that I would be pretty tough when it came to dealing with anyone on station who stepped out of line. I'm pretty affable and easy-going by nature, but I could feel the way things were going and, in hindsight, I probably overstepped the mark, and included a few profanities in my response. But it did the trick, and I got the job, although Ivan did tell me later that one of the interview team made reference during their discussion to the fact that I swore a lot. "Oh, it's OK," Ivan reassured him, "He's from Suffolk. They talk like that round here!" Had my back then, always did.

The inimitable Ivan Howlett. Picture: EADT

The new radio station was to have a brand-new home, Broadcasting House, which was taking shape in Ipswich, replete with a striking turret design at the front, which soon got likened to a rocket! The station's branding was prominent, too. The logo included a plough, the rising sun, and the sea, all clear reminders of the county's heritage, while the station's sound and jingles would be inspired by a beautiful and haunting orchestral work, specially written by the composer, David Arnold.

It was only after a while that it struck me that the building's location - beside the roundabout in St Matthew's Street - was just a few hundred yards from my old primary school, St Matthew's Church of England, at the bottom of the hill. It was there that I was moulded... and slippered, more than once. One incident involved the emptying of a discarded shampoo bottle on the top floor of a bus onto the top of someone's head, who was waiting at the bus stop below. Another for suggesting, when a football got booted over the fence into Civic Drive during a game in the playground, that it would be OK for a fellow pupil to retrieve it. In football parlance, now with VAR, I think both judgements would today be classified as harsh but, in a way, I suppose they helped shape me. I can remember another primary school debacle. I didn't know the meaning of the word at the time, but if I had, I'm sure I would've used it to describe the moment when the headteacher whacked me hard across the back of the head in front of all my peers, in a Lyons tea shop on a trip to London. The accusation - which I've always been comforted to know was completely untrue - was that I'd made some snide comment to another boy, from another school, who rushed to his father to complain. Once the Head had pacified him, he didn't seek to adopt the same passive approach with me but, instead, out of nowhere, came the wallop - and it hurt, rapidly reducing me to tears. I have always, to this day, had a fierce dislike of injustice, and I have no doubt from where it emanated. An innocent victim - for once - at such a tender age. The Head seemed to take great delight in informing my mother all about my alleged misdemeanour the instant we arrived back at school by coach, and how I'd brought shame on everyone. I told her the truth and that nothing had happened. Thankfully, I had the backing of friends who'd been with me at the time and saw it all.

I was undoubtedly a reasonably intelligent child, and I really should've spotted much earlier this developing trend of getting myself into scrapes, through failing to keep my ideas to myself, or failing to keep my mouth shut, or a combination of the two. Alas, the Eureka moment eluded me but, as I prepared to take the reins in this new role, just a stone's throw from where it all began, I couldn't help but think that I hadn't done badly, in hindsight, to scale to these relatively lofty heights. Anyway, back to the building and, inside, it was state-of-the-art. Two identical studios, side by side, which could be viewed by people in Reception, through a glass window. The studio desks were something to behold. Brand new and glistening. Like the flight-deck on an aircraft. More switches, buttons and faders than you could possibly ever need to tug, tap or tweak, but impressive nonetheless. They were top-notch at the time, with turntables and CD players!

The building also had a contribution studio on the ground floor to link us and, more importantly, guests from Suffolk, into the wider BBC network, so they could feature either live or pre-recorded on flagship programmes like Radio 4's *Today* programme. There was also a windowless TV studio to produce output for our regional TV station of BBC *Look East*. A specially-painted image showing the Orwell Bridge formed the backdrop for interviews.

Most of the upstairs floor was taken up by the newsroom, which would be my domain and which, in those early days, seemed cavernous, with no furniture or equipment yet on site. I had my own little office in the corner. Essential, Ivan suggested, for privacy when someone needed a reprimand!

Underneath the whole thing, a car park, so tight that its highly-unforgiving concrete supporting columns would, in the months and years ahead, claim many a victim. The sloped entrance outside, which allowed people to access the parking area at the back, was equally treacherous, especially on the way down. We lost count of the bodywork which got damaged and the wing mirrors which parted company with vehicles, in the deceptively narrow gap between the brick walls either side. It happened, invariably, on the way down, when the gradient added a little more speed to the manoeuvre than was helpful and, just when you thought you'd made it out, the inevitable crunch would come.

We made regular trips to the site to check on progress but most of our time, in those earliest days, was spent working from a modest office in a complex for small firms, about a ten-minute walk away.

As well as Ivan and me, there was Jim Ensom, who was Programme Organiser, David Cox, who was head of Engineering, and Ross Young, who was Administrator, Finance and Personnel.

Ivan was, like me, Suffolk born and bred. A Lavenham boy, he was passionate about the county, its heritage, its people. He always said that being picked as the man who would launch the station here had been his dream job, and it showed every second you were privileged enough to be by his side. More driven than anyone I've ever seen. Passionate about journalism, education, sport, the arts, he was the most wonderful company, and prone to delightful moments of eccentricity. He would invariably burst through the newsroom door, searching me out with an idea, and with a cry of "Hey Mister!" He loved radio. Loved the team. Loyal beyond words.

He knew exactly where Radio Suffolk should slot into the broadcasting landscape, given that there were already three existing and well-established BBC local radio stations on every border, not to mention a strong commercial presence in Radio Orwell, who had developed a fine reputation for their local news output.

So, the challenge for me was to convince the local movers and shakers that Suffolk actually needed us. It was all very well the BBC deciding it did but, on the ground, in some quarters, it was a hard sell, and it wasn't just about making sure people knew we were here, but making sure that the news flowed in. Establishing systems and contacts, compiling a style guide and a comprehensive pronunciation list of place-names, so that, when the new team came on board, they'd know their Bramford (Brarm-fud) from their Bramfield (Bram-field) and their Grundisburgh (Gruns-braa) from their Groton (Grow-tun). Some, however, always remained ill-defined. The River Stour - as in tour, or tower? The answer to that depends in which part of the county you live, but both are correct, although be prepared for a vigorous debate!

There was a huge amount for us to think about but, of course, the most critical element was recruitment. Building the right news team from scratch. We wanted experience. Strong journalists who knew the patch, knew the issues and knew a story; how to find it; how to tell it. But we also needed raw talent to develop, and there was no shortage of that. The chance to work on a brand-new BBC local radio station was a rare opportunity, and they knew it. In Ivan's words, we just slipped under the door before it slammed shut. Every aspect of funding was under scrutiny. We were lucky.

As a management team, we all had things, important things, we needed to be doing, so it was a somewhat alien series of long, long days, when we sat cocooned in the Editor's office, first sifting through piles of applications, and then whittling them down to a shortlist. The interviews were often, by their very nature, tense affairs, but we knew collectively what we wanted more than anything else. Energy, ideas, that little spark in the eyes that said the applicant was up for the challenge and would, most vitally of all, be a good addition to the team. Pulling together would be at the core of everything.

Tense, yes, but also funny. Ivan had a habit of tapping his pencil on the table if he and the interviewee didn't click straight away, and he had an instinctive knack of spotting a problem almost instantly. So, once the tapping began, we knew to push things along!

I had to throw a few legal googlies their way. You think a story is risky and libellous, but a senior producer says run it anyway. What would you do? Or, you've been at a preliminary hearing at magistrates' court. The bench was given plenty of detail about the case and the defendant's previous offences, to help them decide whether to grant them bail, as they handed the matter up to the crown court. How much of that can you use? Would you back yourself, or run it past the duty lawyer?

I'd always loved media law. Its complexity and its ambiguity, and I loved these jousting sessions, as I often teased the journalist on the other side of the table with the suggestion that, yeah, well the lawyer would say that wouldn't they?! Or, the lawyer's not free, and your bulletin is now two minutes away - I need an answer!

One of my other favourite questions at the board was, "What's your greatest weakness?" The cute, but rather contrived, response would be something like, "I'm a perfectionist," or, "People say I'm too kind," or "I drive myself far too hard." So, it was hats off to the candidate who responded with "Chocolates!"

The other thing which this intensive interviewing stint proved, beyond doubt, is that old thought that you have a window of something like seven seconds to make an impression. We saw people blow it sometimes before they'd even reached the chair. Inordinate fear in the eyes, poor body language, the most awful opening pitch. By contrast, of course, others nailed it absolutely in that short space of time. Invariably with their confidence, their smile, their humour. One even impressed by revealing that he didn't have his own tie, so borrowed his grandad's. We remain colleagues to this day!

Eventually, then, the team were assembled, and off they went to the BBC's centre at Grafton House in London, for an intensive spell of training in all aspects of local radio.

As a management team, we would head down later once they'd had time to gel and, when we did, it was wonderful to see the bonds they'd built and, in some cases, see the people who hadn't struck you initially as natural leaders emerge as just that. We also got to make a group visit to see Terry Wogan's evening chat show of the time go out live, and it was only while we were milling about backstage that we detected the smell of cigar smoke, and the man himself appeared, puffing away. Charming, genial and so generous with his time.

Back on station, the moment was fast approaching when we'd be going on air, and so we started dummy runs to make sure the teams worked - the kit worked! One of the most critical areas was the central bench in the newsroom, on which two tape machines sat which would receive the audio material from London, which we could mix in with the local material we were producing. It operated on an auto-start – unless, of course, someone flicked the switch off and forgot to put it back. Result? Entire audio circuit missed. Panic. London also fed up a copy service called "rip-n-read", which was equally vital, until the paper jammed, or ran out at the critical time!

I'd always been belt-and-braces in my approach and, while we were working on a relatively new computer system, I insisted that we had a few manual typewriters tucked away on the top of a cupboard. As I recall, I don't think we ever used them, but that wasn't the point! At least I felt reassured.

And then, it was here. Thursday, 12th April 1990. Ivan wouldn't risk going live on what, to many, was the obvious launch day, the Friday the 13th - so Thursday it was. I can remember that moment like it was yesterday. It started with that wonderful orchestral station theme, and then on came Ivan, the consummate professional; but, to those of us who knew him well, the voice betrayed the enormity of that moment. Nervous. Who wouldn't be? All those hopes and fears, ambition, anxiety. But the lines he delivered were, as ever, eloquent, beautifully written and read. The breakfast show presenter, Chris Opperman, was next up. A big man, with a huge presence, he too was feeling it. Like all of us, this was the moment he'd been waiting for. Countless run-throughs to this, the cold reality. Wagons roll. We were away. Finally let loose on Joe Public.

From that moment, it was all about building the reputation, and in that we were hamstrung initially. FM only. The second biggest town in Suffolk - Lowestoft - couldn't even hear us. A community there which already felt on the fringe of so many things, how on earth could we convince them that they were part of this great adventure too? It was something on which Ivan would need to battle relentlessly to make people realise that this patchwork coverage was totally unacceptable for him - for listeners.

As a news team, we had our work cut out. A breakfast programme which was all-speech, and during the day; what they called big "shoulders of speech" to fill. Half an hour at one o'clock and a one-hour news programme at Drivetime. Producers had to be incredibly resourceful, building up a comprehensive list of contacts who'd be happy for a call - even at some unearthly hour of the morning - to be on air in a flash to react to breaking stories.

Remember, too, this was the age of the cart machine. No highly-automated play-out system. I can still see vividly the sight of one of the news producers, heading into the news booth gripping a stack of nine or ten cartridges nervously between their hands, hoping the whole lot of them didn't slip away, crashing to the floor, before they made it safely to the sanctuary of the studio to present the main bulletin at one o'clock.

It wasn't the only potential pitfall. The carts were of varying lengths - from twenty seconds to three and a half minutes. If supplies of the shorter carts were getting low, sometimes a brief piece of audio would, by necessity, have to be recorded onto one of the long ones. This was OK, until it came to checking the reports before you went on air - something known as pre-fade - where you'd listen to them one by one to ensure that they contained the right audio, that it played OK, and that the cart would re-cue to the correct starting-point, so it would be ready to play once you went live. But, if time was running short, and you'd been forced to use a longer cart, it was very easy to try to re-cue it, which clearly took a lot longer - sometimes, an eternity, and it would still be noisily whirring round as the presenter downstairs handed to you for the bulletin, which left you padding as much as you could until you heard that precious "clonk", as the cart in the slot finally got back to its starting point. Sometimes, if it was a really dodgy longer cart, it would just keep whirring and refuse to stop completely!

For the bulletin readers, on air on their own, it was fraught with problems and, remember - this was a time when, in the field, we were recording interviews and other material onto portable, reel-to-reel tape recorders called Uhers, which had a nasty habit of chewing tape up in the wheels of the recording mechanism. The nightmare for every reporter was to finally stop recording what they thought was a piece of absolute brilliance, only to flip open the plastic Uher lid to reveal a tangled mess! Sometimes it would unravel, sometimes not!

If you got the material safely back to base, you'd edit what was called the "package" together on big reel-to-reel machines, using *Chinagraph*, razor blades and splicing tape. My word, that's a lost art form. Using a *Chinagraph* pencil, you'd mark up the tape at the start and end of the section you wanted to whip out, by laying it delicately into a metal block on the machine, and then cut it with a blade through an angled slot. Remove the duff bit and stick it back together. Simple in theory, but actually really complex, especially when you lost track of which bit you were keeping or losing, from the selection of strips of tape which would invariably end up draped around your shoulders, or on the side of the machine, supposedly for safekeeping. You could always put it back the wrong way round, which was entertaining. Sometimes the critical bit of tape would fall to the floor and end up getting chewed around the wheel on the office chair. It was a process which required real discipline and concentration and, once the edit was complete, you'd add a short length of yellow tape to the start of a piece, to allow it to be laced-up on the spool of the machine, and red tape on the end, to signify the end. It ensured a very clean start and finishing point.

Sometimes, infuriatingly, a piece of yellow or red tape - onto which nothing could record - would be left right in the middle of a reel of tape, which you'd grab in a hurry from the special box of reclaimed spools and, as you'd recorded your interview, you could see it getting closer and closer to the recording heads of the machine, until it sailed nonchalantly through, inevitably right at the moment when your interviewee delivered the best line of the whole interview!

Always makes me smile today, when I think of the ease with which we now edit material together on computers. No drama. No sliced fingers. Nothing mangled. Rarely is anything irretrievable. Everything normally can be undone with a keystroke.

The newsroom at BBC Radio Suffolk. Picture: EADT

Things rarely stood still in the BBC. Computer systems in the newsroom changed. The Uhers went to make way for smaller, digital recorders. The gramophone decks disappeared from the studios; eventually the cart machines and CD players would be consigned to history, too, as everything the presenter could ever need all popped up on a computer screen. Play-out made simple - to a degree.

Systems were always updating and staffing, too, would ebb and flow. Being a new station, we had an incredibly stable team for a reasonably long time, but then people started to move on, to fresh challenges and more senior roles elsewhere, either within the BBC, or outside of the corporation. I knew it was inevitable, to be expected, but I felt such a mix of emotions, especially during those early departures. Proud to see them flourish yet further, but sad to see what we'd created start to fragment.

The output was what mattered most, and it had, we all felt, earned a reputation as both credible and critical for the community.

We acquitted ourselves well in covering major stories, such as the case of Jason Mitchell, a paranoid schizophrenic who, just before Christmas 1994, killed three people at Bramford, including his father. The detail was awful. The ramifications clear. This was a man with a long history of mental disturbance who had been committed, indefinitely, to a secure mental institution in 1990 after an earlier bout of violence - attacking a church cleaner with a baseball bat. But he was later released for care in the community, after a psychiatrist had described him as "a pleasant young man, with no real malice in him." "SUCH A NICE TRIPLE KILLER" was how one newspaper chose to headline the case at the time.

The message from the police in Suffolk had consistently been that such crimes were rare, in what remained a relatively safe county. No doubt that's why this story, and others that would follow - as detailed in later chapters - proved so shocking to the community, which perhaps felt somehow isolated from, and immune to, such violence. But what they did achieve was to sweep away, once and for all, the notion that Suffolk was a slow, sleepy county where nothing ever really happened.

News is neatly defined as that which is furthest from the norm, and so it would prove over and over.

Like all organisations, the BBC was always evolving. Yes, the core pillars of informing, educating and entertaining remained the same, but the three-way balance changed, depending on who was in charge at the top, and what they wanted to hear emanating from the network of local radio stations. It meant that we went through phases when, to my ear, it all felt a bit too analytical. The mission to explain in overdrive. Conversely, there were times when the mood music changed, literally. We were after the mythical pairing of Sue and Dave - they were the listeners we should have in our sights. It was more about being laid back, loose, laughter.

We certainly always tried to have fun, no matter what policy percolated down from on high, and nowhere was that more evident than Children in Need week. In those early days, when we were trying to really make our mark, this festival of feelgood fund-raising was just a joy. The studios at Broadcasting House open for all, as we welcomed them in with open arms, with their giant cheques, their cash, their crazy ways of making money for Pudsey. I remember one year when the theme for CIN night was "summer holidays and the beach." Impressive for a grim night in November. We transformed the outside broadcast garage with palm trees and beach balls, and had a barbecue running, too. Invariably, the TV cameras would also be in that night for all-too-short live updates into the wider BBC, when we'd try to talk to as many visitors as we could, in our given slot - which usually meant a few precious seconds each. It was brief, but brilliant. That building never felt more alive.

Children in Need also triggered highly ambitious projects, as the station tapped deeply into the local community. One year, the goal was to create a play area in Landseer Road in Ipswich, another was to provide a makeover for a building used by youngsters. They were moments when I'd genuinely get close to tears watching the creativity and commitment of so many people bring about real change on our doorstep. Pride beyond words at what the community and the team achieved. It was the heart and soul of local radio's role. Still is today.

Chapter Ten

London Calling

Times were changing. Ivan had decided to step down as Editor, to concentrate on freelance work, and I had a decision to make. They were looking for someone to step into his shoes. Would that someone be me? I had no idea, but I knew I had to try. It wouldn't be an easy process. I'd been with Ivan from the start and I suspected – rightly, as it proved - that they'd want a new broom.

The interview, or board as the BBC calls it, was predictably tricky when the questions came. What would you change? But you've been there long enough, why haven't you made it happen already? Well, um …! The truthful answer was that I had to be loyal to Ivan. It had been his station, after all. It must've sounded weak and näive, even though I truly believed it.

Long story, short. I didn't get it, but I didn't give up. I went for Editor boards at Norfolk and Northampton. Yep, you're right - didn't get them, either. It's at moments like this that you start to see a trend developing and try to reason why. Is the system wrong, or me?

I was quickly saved from what might've proved a rather self-destructive period of soul-searching, by the head of the region, who suggested an "attachment" might be a timely thing. The BBC in London were looking for people to work on the home news-gathering desk at what became known as Stage Six at Television Centre. 24-hour rolling news was looming and this space would be the beating heart of the corporation's news and current affairs teams.

I had nothing to lose and something to gain. A three-month stint in the capital would look good on the CV, so a commuter I became, setting off at some ungodly hour to get to the station in Ipswich, on my little Puch moped. Not always the most reliable of machines, it had a frustrating habit of conking out for no good reason, always when it was raining. Sometimes it was a lost cause but, on the days when I could get it restarted, it meant that, by the time I eventually got into the train carriage, I was soaked, with a wet arse. Delightful company, no doubt, for the fellow-traveller, who presumably wondered why the windows in our section were especially steamed-up! It was a tedious journey even when my arse was bone dry, taking just over an hour, if you were lucky, to make it to Liverpool Street, and then another 45 minutes or so, if you were lucky, before you finally stepped out at White City to gaze upon the iconic, doughnut-shaped structure that I'd seen as a backdrop so often on TV programmes when I was younger.

Through the rotating doors went a steady stream of people - like water flowing through a mill-wheel. Me, I just stood there for a few minutes, taking it all in. Slightly in awe, certainly nervous. I had the feeling that I would be the odd one out, but I quickly realised that a hefty chunk of the BBC's employees were here temporarily, too. Transient. Passing through. On the way - to somewhere!

Inside, the building was clearly in transition too. Large empty spaces, yet to be equipped, but some areas - including the bit where I'd be based - had the basics. Desks, chairs, phones and little gizmo boxes, which you could use to select and monitor everything across TV and radio.

My new boss, Brenda Griffiths, was a joy. An ever-cheery Australian, whose first task on arrival was to make sure that everyone had a coffee and a pastry, available from the number of little wagons dotted around the corridors. Fiercely protective of her team, she was forever reminding us that this corner of the building was a happy place, and it truly was.

At the start of my attachment, I was on the Home Desk, helping pull together the diary for the following day, which would, in many ways, form the starting point for teams across the BBC in TV and Radio. It meant assigning people - reporters, correspondents and producers - and kit - camera crews and satellite vehicles; in short, trying to second-guess what the Gods of News might do, and who and what needed to be where to ensure the programmes, bulletins and, therefore, the audience got everything they needed. It was an incredibly steep learning-curve, understanding the rules of engagement - who did what, which story fell to which team within TVC, and that dictated where you scuttled off to for guidance and advice. Was it Social Affairs, the Legal team, or the Business Unit? Was it a call to the Editors of the various regional bureaux around the country to ensure the geographical spread was right? That old and favourite adage of mine about never assuming anything came to the fore. Together with the belief that there's never a stupid question to ask! But, steadily, I got a grasp of the basics, and I'll never forget the kindness of certain individuals in an environment which could be harsh in the extreme. The Legal Affairs correspondent at the time, Joshua Rosenberg, was one such person, who always had time to help and support you. And then there was Kate Adie, who was this revered figure within the BBC, but who one day appeared beside the Home Desk, as Brenda Griffiths announced proudly that this broadcasting heavyweight had baked a cake and brought some over for us all to enjoy!

I mentioned 24-hour news was looming and, to make sure everything was nailed-down for that, it was critical, not just to include it in our thinking, but to put it front and centre. As well as sorting the nuts and bolts of the news diary, we also worked shifts working on the TV desk, alongside an experienced News Organiser, sitting across the output as it happened and doing the same process of making sure the bodies and bits of kit were precisely where they were needed. As far as rolling news was concerned, we hadn't yet launched on air, so, if it was a shift with News 24, it was dummy runs only. But you wouldn't have known that. It was intense. It had to be, to ensure that, when we did go live, the rivets wouldn't start popping. We all knew how much the BBC was investing in this 24/7 output - in terms of money and reputation - so it had to work and, when it switched from rehearsing to reality, it was remarkably smooth.

I think, at the start, when I was rostered to assist on the desk, I was about as much use as a chocolate fireguard. Things happened at such a frenetic pace, that you had to be switched on from the first moment. The phone would ring constantly. The News Organiser would delegate an ever-changing list of things that needed doing - like NOW! Add to that the sound of squawking voices from production teams on our little comms box, and it was mad.

Ideally, if you'd worked preparing the news diary the day before, you had a head start, because you'd already worked out what might be happening, when and where. But throw into the mix breaking news and the whole thing could quickly become a chaotic maelstrom and, if you weren't totally on your game, a complete and utter mess, which would rapidly draw the venom of the production teams, if they hadn't got the story, reporter, or guest they wanted, when they wanted it.

Half the time, you'd be trying to clarify why a satellite truck hadn't made it from A to B; who'd got the keys to the plug-in point at the Old Bailey; and repeatedly extending line bookings with guest contributors or reporters around the country or the world, apologising for the delay as we battled to slot them into a running order, which was ever-changing. Most days it felt like trying to nail jelly to the wall.

Brenda once told me that my greatest gift was being able to talk common sense, and it was perhaps because of this that she added to my responsibilities by getting me to help prepare the news-gathering diary, not just for the following day, but the entire following week. It meant I had to oversee the pulling-together of story prospects from around the building, and around the country, and set them out in a hastily-stapled-together document, which would be dished out to the plethora of Editors and production teams at a weekly meeting, either held within TVC, or at another venue, such as Bush House, which meant we had to leap into a cab and hoss through the capital.

The one piece of advice which always rang sharply in my ears was that you never replied to anyone in these meetings that you didn't know the answer. So, if someone sought your thinking on what might happen in the coming days in, say, Belfast, where things at that time were still incredibly volatile, you had to explain who needed to be where and when to ensure the BBC could react. My instinct, though, was to be wary of digging myself a huge hole into which I could plunge, so, invariably, I played it belt and braces. Told it the way I saw it, but didn't get silly. These meetings were full of some of the finest editorial brains in the corporation and thankfully, most times, the knack of talking common sense prevailed.

As part of the appraisal system, we were given regular and detailed feedback, which came, anonymously, from those working above and below you, and I well remember one comment - that I was either incredibly calm under pressure, or didn't actually appreciate what was happening around me! Harsh, I thought, but invariably true on those days, when the weight on top of the pressure cooker of news was rattling like crazy. Anyway, spending time panicking and running around like a headless chicken in a crisis had always seemed like wasted time to me, hence the calm exterior!

Brenda, though, had great belief, and soon I'd be working, not just assisting with shifts on the desk, but working as News Organiser myself, invariably through the night. It was a huge responsibility. The first port of call for the BBC across TV and radio when that phone on the desk rang to say the big story had broken. But, thankfully, the big balloon never went up on my watch and, in truth, the hard bit was staying awake on what were long, long shifts. Once you'd paid your umpteenth visit to a café or vending machine, time didn't just drag, it seemed to go backwards. Often, I had to concede defeat and find a comfy corner in which to doze, knowing full well that my pager (remember those?) would ping in an emergency. In fact, one night I was so tired that I fell asleep at the desk, and woke to think that the building was on fire, only to discover that it was the blood-red sunrise, streaming through the vast windows looking out over White City!

What I loved about TVC was that you never knew who you'd bump into - famous faces, from Elton John to Parkinson and Bruce Forsyth - were everywhere - outside by the "doughnut", where the chauffeured cars and cabs used to pull up - in the foyer, or in the lift. For someone like me, who'd always had a knack of spotting a celebrity, it was a joy. But you also never knew where you'd end up. One Friday, Brenda asked me if I could be in Belfast that weekend. It was a critical time in the marching season, and they needed a field producer to help support news output if it all kicked off. The only complication was that I wasn't trained for what was deemed a Hostile Environment, so that task passed me by but, within weeks, I was booked onto the week-long course in Surrey, which everyone talked about, despite being told not to, with the advice to take some rough clothes with you, just in case you get kidnapped.

Sure enough, there we were then - in the classroom, being taught the basics of survival by a team of experts, the majority seasoned ex-military, when we're told that we're breaking into two groups to do an exercise outside. Off we set, loading up into Land Rover vehicles. I climbed in the front. As we set off down a gravel track to one side of the main building, I was just thinking, given our speed, that it would be hairy if we met someone coming the other way, when from the side, from seemingly nowhere, another vehicle cut across us at an angle, blocking our path. At my window, a hooded figure, screaming at us all to get out. We did. Their language was colourful and unnerving. We were pushed roughly to the ground, face down, with more swearing, and hoods made from sacking were placed over our heads. It was very alien, but by far the most troubling thing was having my wedding ring pulled from my finger. All jewellery had to come off.

We were forced to stand - amid more shouting - and then led away - with a hand placed on the shoulder of the person in front. To where, we didn't know, but we were clearly being walked through a wooded area, because branches would suddenly strike my face. The most bizarre, but reassuring thing was how quickly, deprived of sight, the other senses became more intense. Sounds around us like birdsong and voices, as well as distinct smells.

We moved from outside to in and what, to my ear, sounded like an echoey barn. We were made to sit in silence, for what seemed like an eternity, but was probably only a matter of minutes. One in our group started to have what sounded like a panic attack. They were taken away. The problem, we were later told, was down to a mix of asthma and claustrophobia.

What it proved to me was that while a physical, threatening presence can be intimidating, it's the moments of silence which can be the most worrying, when you're unsure what might happen and when, so your mind runs away with random thoughts.

Eventually the hoods came off, and we were, as we'd thought, inside an old building, with our captors - our trainers. Only a simulation, but they knew how to make it real.

We were taught so much in that week. On the rifle range, the deadly impact of a range of firearms, and the safe place to stand behind a rocket-propelled grenade launcher! How to administer life-saving first aid on the frontline. How to spot signs of booby traps and tripwires. And how to avoid being taken hostage, as well as how to handle it if it happens. It all seemed a world away, but we would learn, in the years that followed, that some people on that course would encounter the situation for real in the field. On a wider level, what it did was to remind us that there are plenty of "hostile environments" all around us, often in the most unexpected situations, and being equipped to think about how you handle yourself and the people around you when tensions rise has proved invaluable. I still remember the advice that it's never wise to play the hero, but to try to remain virtually unnoticed, cool and calm. The "grey" ones. They're the ones who invariably make it through.

It also reminded me that I am not cut from the cloth which produces the hard-nosed, war-zone type. I found the sight of a bullet, not just striking, but going right through a steel girder, more than a little disconcerting. The only weapon I'd previously held was an air-rifle as a kid, or a paint-ball gun as a grown-up. But, years later, I would again feel that intense sense of unease when confronted by the reality of what deadly force means, when we were invited to venture inside what they called "the killing house" on one of our military bases. Our American hosts gave us the choice of a sub-machine gun or pistol, as we prepared to move at speed through corridors and into rooms on two floors, knowing that the aim - literally - was to take out the life-size targets which were our assailants, firing paint-tipped bullets. Again, just a simulation, but the idea of having to make that kind of split-second decision for real filled me with dread. No warrior me!

Anyway, back to TVC and, while I'd only meant to stay for a short attachment, my boss, Brenda, clearly liked me and I liked the way she ran things too, so the stint kept getting extended, and I felt more confident as the weeks rolled by. I knew how to navigate my way round the system, I knew how to handle the people, who could often display a hostility in meetings which I found odd. It was hugely competitive. Editors, producers, correspondents, reporters and planners, from both television and radio, all trying to ensure that they, their teams, their audience, didn't miss out on their slice of the news-gathering cake. Raised voices. Heightened emotions. Some were always quick to try to condemn you, others could be tremendously supportive. As always, honesty won. I was never keen to pretend I had all the answers. I didn't, but I sought the answers and counsel from those who did.

Crunch time came. The decision had to be made over whether I would remain at the centre, or return to Suffolk. A post was offered to work as a field producer, which would essentially mean a suitcase and a life on the road for the majority of the time, being parachuted in to grease the cogs of news, wherever and whenever the story broke. London still excited me, but I'd grown tired of commuting, which slowly and steadily wears you down. Too many times I'd sit and stare out of the train-carriage window across the river, as we pulled up at Manningtree station as the sun was setting, or had already disappeared. Almost home, but knowing full well that I'd be up again first thing tomorrow to do the same trek again.

So, I decided against staying on, and returned to work at BBC Radio Suffolk. I had told myself that I would never be back, but here I was, heading up the stairs to the newsroom once more. I'd be working as producer of the breakfast programme and I really did relish it. After the layers of complexity and invariable conflict in London, I loved the simplicity of converting great ideas into great radio really quickly, but I was aware that it was probably better for everyone if I moved on to something else. I didn't want to feel - or be seen - as someone who'd slotted back into something which was safe and comfortable, and having felt that a potential climb up the BBC ladder of management was no longer an option - perhaps because I didn't have the university education for which I think they secretly yearned - I had to think tangents and out of the blue and, thankfully, I landed the plum job.

Chapter Eleven

Cue Kevin!

I'd already worked for a time as a producer at BBC Look East HQ at All Saint's Green in Norwich, trying to hold together the multitude of threads it takes to create a successful 26 minutes or so of live TV every night, and, invariably, on most days, one or more of those strands would break. It often felt inevitable and, when things did go wrong, there was always an inquest. In the days when I was producing, that inquest invariably came on the following day, at the morning news meeting - and if it was a full-on, no-holds-barred session, it wasn't pretty and it certainly wasn't the best way to kick off a new day. Morale quickly hit the floor.

But that's TV. It's a tough, often brutal business. I well remember the first day I walked into the newsroom as a newcomer. The day was wet and so, before leaving home to catch the train to Norwich, I pulled from the car the first waterproof thing I could find - a pink-and-mauve-coloured cagoule - to afford some protection as I scuttled to the office. "Ooh look," shouted some wag, as I walked in - causing all heads to turn in my direction, "Kevin Burch has come in fancy dress!" I couldn't think of a witty riposte, so I shuffled over to my desk. I don't think I ever wore that cagoule to work again.

Producing is all about ideas. Especially on those slow news days, when - despite your best efforts - you begin with a virtually blank page. The ideas need to be run up the flagpole, and invariably and instantly shot down, especially if you haven't really had time to think them through so that they're fully-formed. I used to feel bruised at first but, in the end, I didn't worry too much. It's what happens. Sink or swim.

Close to what?

I think I managed to swim, but only doggy-paddle and barely keeping afloat, so my energy needed directing elsewhere, and that elsewhere was in front of, not behind the camera.

Kevin Bentley was the reporter who covered Suffolk for BBC Look East. He was a pioneer. A true bi-media operator, producing reports for both television and radio. Even the works car was branded differently on either side to reflect this 50/50 split. Kevin worked from a windowless room on the ground floor at BBC Radio Suffolk, equipped with the basics as well as a camera, lights and a suitably-Suffolk backdrop - that bespoke painting of the Orwell Bridge mentioned earlier - for any pieces-to-camera or guest interviews.

I'd worked closely with Kevin. He was larger-than-life - extrovert, energetic, and always looked like he was having fun. So, when he decided to leave to pursue a career in politics, this Kevin applied, and landed the job.

I never expected it to be a stroll in the park, but I was quickly aware just now demanding the role would be. It was before we had the benefit of wi-fi to feed material back, so every story usually required you to charge back to the radio building once filming was complete, and then feed your piece "up the line", using a technique called track and rushes, the track being your voice, and the rushes being your raw, unedited material. It was a task always performed at breakneck speed, with the clock ticking. The feed of rushes would be set rolling, while you hastily thought about what you wanted to say to ensure the perfect marriage of words and pictures - crisp, coherent, clever, if you were lucky. Most days it was a pig's ear! The instant the feed of pictures was over, the editor, producer or VT Co-ordinator at the other end, would be screaming for the track because that, of course, was the thread which would hold the whole thing together. Rarely time to think about what the viewer would be seeing and hearing, and whether the combination would make sense. The priority was simply to get it away.

If you had the advantage of working at All Saints Green itself, the process was simpler, because you would invariably sit alongside an editor to produce the piece, but you still had moments when you felt the heat. The voice had to be laid down in a little booth along the corridor, which got awfully busy the closer we got to the start of the programme at 6.30pm, so you'd often peek through the small, glass window to see another reporter recording at the microphone. When they came out and it was your moment to go in, you never had time to faff about. The editor could talk to you on headphones and, when he or she said go, you went - hoping not to fluff your lines. Tough, but nothing compared to the days when reporters had the added pressure of voicing their films live.

There's an undeniable thrill when you see your first piece go out on the telly, although, looking back on my early work, it all looks a bit too rough and ready. I suspect it's the same for all of us when we're starting out. Areas to work on. Room for improvement. The only difference is that this learning process happens every night, often live, in front of thousands of people sitting at home. The blessing for me - and others who were new to the game - was that we were surrounded by people in the Look East "family" who really knew their craft and who took pleasure in helping you develop, not delight in seeing you struggle. Camera crews who gathered the most exquisite shots, and picture editors who then married those with a few well-chosen lines to create a thing of real beauty. Brevity from the reporter was everything, as you sought the words which would, as the saying goes, "touch" the pictures, and make the process of story-telling succinct and simple. Don't tell the viewer what they can see - enhance what they see with short bursts of thought. Everything is driven by strong, visual images. Start with the strongest. If the story doesn't have pictures, you don't really have a story. But if you have strong pictures and compelling actuality - that's the powerful voices of ordinary people talking... it's a home-run. And sometimes, like your scripting, the shorter the actuality, the better. Contributors can ramble on for thirty seconds and say little, or hit you with the classic nugget, or sound-bite, lasting just a few seconds. Once you hear it, you'll know it, and you might as well pack up there and then. It's priceless.

The first thing that every new reporter gets obsessed about is the piece-to-camera, and I was no different. It's top of the list. So, I was grateful to the camera crews who, with great subtlety, steered thoughts away from what's uppermost in your mind, to what's actually happening right in front of you. The realisation dawned pretty quickly that the piece-to-camera, or PTC, is often nice to have - it shows the viewer that you're out there, doing the business - but it's rarely essential. If it shows something which needs explaining, if it gives a sense of place, or it allows transition from one sequence to another - then all's cool. If not, don't do it. Value, not vanity.

One of the most vivid moments of simple story-telling I remember was the clearance of a travellers' site at Little Waltham in Essex, in 2004. Camera operator John Nichols and I arrived early. The first things we noticed were large gas bottles. I think, from memory, it was propane, dotted along the edge of the site which fronted the road, behind a shallow ditch, which the travellers had dug to try to prevent, or certainly slow, any vehicles getting on to the site. There were a few officials in the road and, from within the site, behind the hedging, we could hear voices from the travellers themselves. That initial scan didn't reveal too much about the scale of the operation which was about to unfold. After a court battle costing £100,000, and three years after the travellers had bought the plot of land – but, critically, didn't initially seek planning permission

- bailiffs working on behalf of the borough council, supported by the police, were going in to clear the site.

But when we took a wander beyond the bend further down the road, the sight of a mini-army of people, all kitted out in helmets and protective kit, and a long line of vehicles stretching back as far as we could see, left us in no doubt that this would be full-on and fast.

Walking back, we saw the reasons for the gas bottles, as one of the travellers turned on one of the valves and warned the officials, over the sound of a menacing hiss and with lighter in hand, what would happen if they tried to force their way in.

But that stand of defiance counted for little, as the bailiffs started to march forward, behind a large digger, over the ditch and towards the travellers' homes.

We followed behind them, at what felt a safe distance until, in a split second, the official in front of us, who was built pretty substantially, hit the floor like a sack of coal. As the group advanced, a youngster had manoeuvred behind us, and was throwing lumps of rubble at the backs of the men. Ahead of us, a 4x4-type vehicle began slewing in our direction, through the quagmire of mud. John and I decided pretty rapidly that this was now too risky and we retreated back to the road, from where we could still see and film the bailiffs kicking down fencing and trashing flower beds; in short, flattening pretty much anything which stood in their way. The travellers could do little and, afterwards, spoke of their frustration and anger, while officials reflected on a show of force which had, in their eyes, become their only option.

Memories of that day would be rekindled on 19th October 2011, at Dale Farm, also in Essex, when 80 families were evicted from homes which had been illegally built on the land. It was, at the time, Europe's largest traveller site, and the eviction was the culmination of a seven-year battle, with the travellers and their supporters demanding permission to remain, claiming they had nowhere to go, while Basildon Council and residents insisted that planning law had to be upheld in the face of what they saw as a massive breach. The fight would go all the way to the House of Lords, but it ended with the bailiffs and police - clad in riot gear - clearing the illegal plots.

It'd been odd watching the mood change in the months leading up to that moment. I'd been to Dale Farm several times to interview the families there, and always been well received. There was natural suspicion. There always is when a camera's involved, but there were key figures on site who you'd call beforehand and who would, invariably, be happy to talk. After all, they were being backed into a corner and needed us to tell their side of the story. I remember sitting in one of their caravans as they played host to Lord Avebury, the Liberal Democrat peer. It was the most glorious September day, the sun streaming through the windows and, laid out before us, the most wonderful buffet. It's funny the things you remember, but I do recall that some of the sandwiches were filled with grated cheese and, despite the best efforts of the guests, the cheese invariably kept spilling out onto the carpet whenever one was picked up. Every time it did, one of the family members would scuttle in to clear it up. They were incredibly houseproud and the most amiable hosts. Everyone there spoke with passion. Everyone there believed this was a fight they could win. But, in the weeks that followed, it felt to me as if the travellers themselves drifted more into the background, their places taken by activists, who established an increasing presence at the main gate and were keen to ensure that they were the ones who'd handle contact with the media.

But any contact became even more limited because, with tensions rising, the council had built a vast compound beside the site. The ground covered with metal sheeting and the whole area protected by high fencing. You had to phone through the day before to tell them that you were coming and then, on arrival, get yourself signed in. Any interviews - usually with the council leader - had to be undertaken at a safe distance back from the fence adjacent to the site itself. Far enough back, security told us, to be out of the range of missiles such as bricks and bottles, just in case. The debris littering the floor told you that they spoke from experience.

Come the day of the eviction itself, and it wasn't just the council and police who were there in force, but the media, too, who love an underdog and were keen to witness what was building up to be a battle between David and Goliath. The BBC had, quite rightly, taken risk assessment incredibly seriously, so we were each assigned our own security minder, who'd be with us at all times. Ours was a hugely reassuring presence from the off, telling me that he had a knack for spotting, through eyes and body-language, the people who'd pose a clear threat, and when I asked, naively, how I'd know if trouble was brewing, he suggested it would be pretty obvious, as I'd be moving backwards at a rate of knots, with him yanking the belt of my trousers!

During operations like this, the key is always to strike fast, in numbers and early, so it was dawn when the first police teams went in, breaking down a fence at the rear of the site to gain entry and then swarming through in numbers.

We were positioned close to the main entrance, where a high, scaffolded barricade had been built, and reinforced with wooden pallets, metal sheets, in fact, anything the protesters could lay their hands on. All around us were banners. One read "Stop The Eviction", but, in truth, they could do little to resist the wave of numbers now flooding the site, the air filled with drifting, thick, black smoke from the bonfires which were now burning all around. There was shouting and screaming, too, riot shields being struck repeatedly by a salvo of bricks, rocks and bottles. There was also the light, crackling sound of a taser being shot to subdue.

Some of the families at Dale Farm had upped and left before eviction day, knowing all too well what the outcome would be, and now, with chaos all around them, others were fleeing. One of the most telling images from the day was that of a woman running away from the conflict with a child in her arms.

Like the police and bailiffs, we had a job to do, so we moved back once more to the safety of the council compound. Gradually the adrenaline, the fear we felt - even with the reassuring presence of a minder by our side - started to subside and we began the process of distilling down what we'd seen and heard. It's at times like this that you slip effortlessly into the task of telling the story. Best pictures first, always - tracing the chronology of the day and using as pointers those journalistic basics of what? where? when? how? and why? I was always taught at the newspaper to write stories with an inverted triangle in mind. The word WHAT running down it vertically. What's happened, How it's happened, then Amplification, then Trivia. That way, we were told, the most important facts always led the way and, if the story had to be cut, the subs could start from the bottom and work their way up, and none of the vital information got lost.

It was a mindset which always served me well and, as the script was written, it flowed. Letting the imagery dictate; minimal words, more bursts of thoughts - touching the pictures and guiding the viewer through the timeline. And, as so often, the stories you write quickly, without too much time to ponder, are the best. Frequently I've gone back to try to re-cut a film which has been constructed in haste to meet the deadline for an earlier bulletin, only to conclude that tweaking would be superfluous. It contains everything that's needed. Leave be.

And so it was at Dale Farm; and only on the drive home did the legs start to wobble, as I reflected on how unsettling the past few hours had been. Important to be there, as a witness to see it unfold. No winners or losers, just conflict. Ugly conflict, but inevitable once all the talking and legal to-ing and fro-ing had been exhausted.

In all, there were 45 arrests, with injuries on both sides. The cost to the council, for the eviction itself and the legal fight which preceded it, ended up close to £7 million. The bill for policing was £2.3 million.

Compared to what I saw at the earlier traveller clearance at Little Waltham, this was on a different scale, but I would cross paths with travellers many more times during my reporting work. One happened at Kesgrave four years later, in July 2015. Tensions had been building, with rumours rife that up to 100 were on their way and planning to set up camp on an area of open space.

Locals blocked the verges with cars and wheelie bins, desperate to keep them at bay by sealing-off potential routes onto grassed areas.

When I arrived, there was a group of about a dozen caravans, pitched-up behind a local pub. Some of the younger members were sitting on the picnic tables, beers open, more supplies on hand. It was not long after 9am. They, understandably, eyed me cautiously. But I always sought to show respect, to stress that I was here to get their side of the story and, most essential of all, to identify very quickly the senior figure in the group, who would speak on behalf of the families.

In this case, I was pointed towards an older man sitting at a picnic table, also loaded with plenty of beer bottles - both empty ones and full ones - and what also caught my eye, not unsurprisingly, was the glint of a kitchen knife sitting there too, which I quickly found out was being used to whip off the caps of the bottles and, potentially I feared, the end of someone's finger.

Nevertheless, the older man was happy to talk to explain that one of their number had needed hospital treatment and they were waiting until that was resolved before moving on. There was talk of a Christening, too, at the local Catholic Church.

He said he fancied a walk, so got up, and I followed alongside him. We hadn't gone more than a few yards, when he asked me if I had a car. I said yes. Good, he told me, because they needed more alcohol and he suggested I could act as driver! It was at that precise moment that I realised this had the potential to become, very quickly, a tricky negotiation to resolve. I didn't fancy taking on a beer run, but I didn't want to offend him, either. I obviously had to stand my ground, so I said no and, clearly feeling badly let down by my refusal to play ball, he turned on his heel, muttering, and headed back to the others.

But we'd meet again, outside the church, when they duly turned up for the Christening, a much smaller gathering than had been rumoured, all dressed in their finery and looking utterly fabulous, the children especially chattering with unbridled excitement. The man paused to talk to me through the car window as soon as he arrived, explaining that the hospital treatment had been sorted, and that they'd soon be on their way. He told me on camera that he was genuinely sorry if local people had felt alarmed, and he was quick to apologise.

The bulk of the travellers moved off soon after, but still there was disquiet from residents, complaining that rubbish and debris had been left behind at the spot where they'd stayed, so I returned. This time, there were only a couple of caravans, and black sacks which it seemed had been filled with litter, and police were patrolling the perimeter. As I made my way across to one of the caravans, the door opened and out leapt a small, terrier-type dog, which charged towards me. Now I like dogs, but not this one, especially once he sank his teeth into the leg of my trousers. This kind of thing always happens when you've just invested in a new suit, and this one, which the mutt was seriously trying to shred, was but a few days old. I asked the woman peering out of the door if she might call him off, to which she responded, "It's not his fault. He doesn't know who you are!"

Eventually, he relented, and she told me that they'd be gone within the hour. They were. The trousers were only mildly gnawed. Glamorous life? Nah. Not a bit of it!

While at Look East, I also had a bash at presenting, which was fun, albeit a bit too much of a straitjacket if I'm honest, where every bulletin, every single link and item, was nailed-down to the split second. But it was a chance to perform on the Look East set in Norwich, and wear make-up. I was always reassured that it was necessary, to prevent that sweaty look under the heat of the studio lights, but it still felt odd slapping it on. In fact, the whole process is rather bizarre. An earpiece ensures you can hear the director, who tells you when to start talking and, more importantly, the person who's timing the whole thing, so you know precisely how long you have before you're back in vision, or need to wrap things up. When I started doing it, the autocue, which brings up the words you need to read on the camera to which you're working, was controlled by someone else but, increasingly, you had to operate it yourself using a small pedal under the desk, a bit like an accelerator. With practice, you could whizz through all the items to rehearse and then reset it, to take you back to the start, ready for the off. Once you went live, you could adjust the speed of the flow of words, so it appeared a thing of beauty. However, even with the utmost care, it was very easy, when you were under pressure and had dashed into the studio with seconds to spare, to get it all horribly wrong and lose your way. I can only liken it to hurtling off a treadmill in the gym, when you inadvertently put the machine onto max, when what you really wanted was the setting for a leisurely warm-up! It was the stuff of nightmares. A recurring one at night saw me stumble into the studio having forgotten my scripts and finding that nothing is where it should be and nothing works, which means you had to ad-lib your way through the bulletin, with a deranged director screaming in your earpiece to just keep going. And just when you thought it couldn't get any worse, you look down and realise that you're completely naked! The real thing could be bizarre too, though. I remember one occasion when the delightful Julie Reinger, who regularly presented the weather for Look East, wandered across the studio before we went live, and whispered something in my ear. Now, to be honest, that would've been a lovely moment, except that I'm slightly deaf in one ear and, with my earpiece located firmly in my other, I couldn't hear a thing. So she repeated it. Once more, I couldn't hear, and so I did that terribly British thing of just laughing, thinking it was some quip. Now confused by my inability to display any kind of recognition of what she'd said, Julie tried for a third time - still no joy. It was only later, with the earpiece out and my hearing roughly somewhere back near normal, that Julie told me that she'd been trying to warn me that, as I prepared to go live to the Eastern Region, I'd been sitting with my flies undone! I'm sure no one noticed, but did I feel a fool or what?

Working with Julie was always fun. Once you strike up a good relationship on screen, producers like to repeat the trick, and I remember one outside broadcast at Southwold Lighthouse, where the plan was that I'd be at ground level, doing a bit of business about the structure, its history, etc., and then I'd hand to Julie, who'd be at the very top and would present the weather. While she was doing that, I'd run up the steps and we'd be reunited on high by the time she'd finished. Well, that was a cracking idea in theory but, when we decided to test it out, we realised that this magnificent, 102-foot-tall landmark had a total of 113 steps in its spiral staircase, and to try to whizz up them all in the time we'd have would be nigh impossible, even for Usain Bolt. (He actually wasn't around at that point, but you get my drift). There was another problem, too. Having walked leisurely to the top with the lighthouse-keeper to get a feel for what we might be able to do, when I went to venture outside onto the concrete cap my legs went to absolute jelly. "You OK?" he asked, adding that this was the point when some people discovered that the ability to do so much as move an inch eluded them, and the desire to just cling on to the circular metal rail mattered more than life itself. "I've been better," I think I replied, as he was attempting to show me some of the key features in the panoramic vista now on offer from this lofty perch. Suggesting that the inside was, for me, now a far better place to be, we did just that. He was very understanding, thankfully.

Back at ground level, I explained the change of plan to Les Ward, the camera operator, who didn't seem surprised, as he'd noted, while zoomed-in on my face as I'd emerged at the summit, a sudden change in colour to deathly pale. Needless to say, I stayed on the green between the lighthouse and the brewery and Julie did the daring bit. Altitude and attitude, what a trouper!

The secret formula of Look East was its warmth. The audience loved the fact that the main presenters and reporters felt real, were real. We had a totally professional approach to everything that we did, but we also had fun, and I like to think that the viewers saw us as one big family, to which they also belonged. It was why the viewing figures and level of appreciation remained so high. We were, after all, popping up in their front rooms most nights of the week. Informed, informal and, most importantly, familiar. Like good friends. They felt they knew us and understood us, and that pre-existing level of trust, which was so vital in covering local news, proved invaluable time and again, but especially when you turned up unannounced on someone's doorstep. Nevertheless, away from work, people could sometimes be frozen with fear once they realised who you were, especially if they stumbled upon you shopping or doing other everyday things, seemingly mystified that you also needed to get the essentials done. Others, though, adopted a no-holds-barred approach. One viewer spotted me walking the dog one morning and shouted across the local park, "Blimey, size of you, I'd thought you'd be running!" Some could be complimentary; "Ooh, you look even better in the flesh!" Others less so. "You're a lot bigger than I thought. Have you put on weight?!" You had to take it all with good grace. As the actor Richard Gere once said, if you believe the good stuff, you have to believe the bad stuff too, so best to ignore it all!

I loved the bond which existed between us and the general public and between us, within the team. Many of us had worked together for some years. Take Susie Fowler-Watt, for instance. We first met when she came to work at Radio Suffolk when I was News Editor, as a fresh-faced reporter, and was posted to cover the Lowestoft area. It wasn't everyone's cup of tea, working pretty much in isolation in a patch as far removed from the centre of things as you could get. But Susie excelled, and we still laugh today about our very first district office there, tucked away in the corner of the local council housing office, where the sound of the toilet cistern re-filling behind the wall could compromise many an interview! Humble beginnings, eh?

Live outside broadcasts, or OBs as we'd call them, were also rarely uneventful, for the simple reason that, when people see a camera - especially with a bright light on top - it is inevitably like moths to a flame. There was a time when, generally, people would just leave you to get on with it, treating it with a degree of respect and reverence. But, increasingly, they felt the need to get in on the action, even if the best they could offer was the ubiquitous, "Hello Mum!" or by inquiring, "Can I be on the telly?" to which the answer was always no! If you do fancy securing a walk-on part, my advice would always be, subtlety! Just wander in to the shot, discreetly. Any more than that, especially inane grinning or gurning, will almost certainly never see the light of day. I remember one live piece we did from Braintree early on in my TV career; it was a Friday night and, as soon as we arrived in the Market Square, we knew that there'd be trouble. People were sitting outside the pubs and bars, clearly well-oiled and, having spotted the arrival of the evening's entertainment, were intent on getting noticed. We had about 45 minutes before we were going on air and, as we were sitting in the OB truck, there was constant banging on the outside. We had a decision to make and there seemed only one option - to present our bit from the balcony of the town hall, which would at least give us the feeling of being outside, while protected from any interruptions. It was a good job we did because, come the moment, come the crowd, including one who was still intent on dropping his tracksuit bottoms and mooning at us as we spoke warmly about some of the attractions this place had to offer!

I always dreaded the call from the producer to tell you that an outside broadcast was planned, either in a busy public place or a pub, and they needed someone to act as producer on site, which was normally code for pretending to be security. Now I'm not trained in the art of diffusing trouble, but I am pretty good at sensing trouble. I remember working on a live with Stewart White in a pub on a Friday night in Clacton. We were just about to go on air, and the crowd inside, although in high spirits, were all as good as gold. Then a guy walked in and, spotting his mates, let fly with a torrent of swearing. Realising we'd just dodged a bullet by a split second, and seeing his eyes light up at the sight of Stewart, the cameras and lights, I could pretty much read his mind so I moved in and explained what all the fuss was about. For the next 20 minutes or so, we chatted like old mates about life, about his desperately sad family situation, about his kids - "Who I'm sure love you?" "No they don't, they hate me!" and how drink was his only friend. He didn't really need to tell me that, because by now I was feeling somewhat intoxicated myself, just through the alcoholic fumes on his breath, as he ranted on, our faces just inches apart. In truth, as in so many situations, he really only wanted to talk, so we did, until the danger had passed and I wished him well and thanked him for being so courteous. I think he looked upon me as his new-found counsellor. Never a dull minute!

This knack of hiding the matches before people had a chance to light the blue touch paper was something those around me had, too. So many times I'd see camera crews using smart diversionary tactics to provide alternative entertainment. When the cry went up from another well-oiled passer-by once, on a job in Ipswich, "Look there's Susie - I'm gonna get on the telly!", a swift intervention steered him away. An invitation to have a look inside the satellite vehicle and see what was going on in there, with all its high-tech wizardry, was a sure-fire winner.

Frequently, when faced with that recurring question ahead of a live - "What are you up to, mate?" we'd insist that we were simply recording something for later, or waiting for further instructions from the centre and suggest, politely that they'd be better off heading home and watching it on the TV later. They soon got bored hanging around, so invariably it worked.

Sometimes there would be security with us. Some were invaluable, as mentioned earlier during the major traveller eviction in Essex but, often, they were little more than a hindrance. I remember one night in Ipswich working with a "specialist", who made all the right noises and reassured me that we had nothing to fear with him around. The only problem was that, when the friction came, from a guy who was extremely vocal and threatening to get violent unless we stopped filming, because we weren't welcome, the specialist was nowhere to be seen. Once the atmosphere had calmed, he suddenly reappeared from behind a bush and resumed his position at my shoulder to tell me that if anything had kicked off, "I'd have taken him out, just like that." Not always what you need when a firm but passive approach seems to work well enough!

I remember another day, near Stowmarket, when I was filming, on my own, a story about a drive to stop people at the local shopping area parking in bays intended for drivers with disabilities. It was a no-nonsense crackdown, involving the use of cctv cameras. As I was working, a car pulled up and the lad who got out of the passenger side was clearly fired-up, insisting on knowing what I was doing, that I had no right to film him which, I reassured him, I hadn't. It was first thing in the morning, but he was wide-eyed and agitated, standing inches from my face and refusing to back away. He then unloaded a torrent of abuse both at me and about the BBC, suggesting we were all corrupt and couldn't be trusted. I told him this didn't feel like the time or the place for that kind of debate and, while he was entitled to his opinion, it might be best if he cracked on with his shopping, which was like a red rag to a bull. How dare I tell him what to do?!

I tried to carry on, while putting space between us, but he wouldn't budge until, finally, he backed away, telling me that he would come back for me later with a weapon. He never did but, to be honest, it's the kind of thing which leaves you worried and wondering - what if…?

As I stood there, trying to work out what on earth had just happened in what felt like the least hostile setting in the world - outside the local Co-op - a man wandered over to reassure me that he'd filmed the whole thing on his phone and was equally perplexed over what provoked such an onslaught. We swapped contact details and he promised to send me the footage, which he did within the hour. It was disturbing to watch it back again, and that's the lesson. When things kick off, they kick off really quickly. It's unpredictable. Unnerving. Goes with the turf. I don't, though, want to give the impression that people mean problems. Far from it. The majority of those I've met on the road have been caring and kind. Prepared to go to extraordinary lengths to offer help and support, often in adversity. Those are the moments and the memories which are to be cherished. The decency of the unsung.

Chapter Twelve

Celebrity

I mentioned my early brushes with celebrities, notably Michael Palin on the prom in Southwold, but many more would follow down the years, and it's always a favourite question - who's the most famous person you've met? Well I suppose, for this generation, Ed Sheeran would be nailed-on, and the moment in 2015 when he received an honorary degree from the University of Suffolk for his "outstanding contribution to music." I was there only to ensure the filming and interview went smoothly, but what struck me was that, while he was probably, at that stage, the biggest name in music, he looked relaxed and humble. Chatting away to our presenter, Susie, posing for pictures, he even signed a guitar which our camera operator, John Fairhall, had recently got for his son and brought along on the off-chance that Ed might add his autograph. He did. Raking in millions, but a really nice guy. Gifted, but grounded.

One of my proudest bits of work was producing a half-hour documentary to mark the passing of the local legend that was Sir Bobby Robson, the former Ipswich and England manager. Talk about a hero! I was 18 when he guided Town to that iconic Wembley win over Arsenal in the FA Cup in 1978, and 21 when UEFA Cup glory came in 1981. So, to be chatting to the likes of Wembley goal-scorer Roger Osborne and team-mates Kevin Beattie and Mick Mills about what made that man special, was the stuff of dreams. I remember meeting Robson when he first came back to Portman Road as manager of Newcastle United. I called him to arrange an interview for that night's Look East. He sounded prickly. He was meant to be playing golf. I suggested we could meet later at his house. "No," he said firmly, "we'll do it at the

Marlborough Hotel," which has now disappeared, but used to stand in the town's Henley Road. "Great," I said, "I'll call them." "No you won't," he said, "I'll do it!" So, later that day, I duly arrived, fearing that Robson perhaps wouldn't be enamoured of the prospect of indulging the local TV station with an interview in the hotel gardens. But no, not a bit of it. He was a delight; in fact, as we walked from the cars to the rear of the building, we were greeted by the sight of a beautiful plant - I think it might have been a magnolia - and so we started talking about the beauty of flowers, Robson bemoaning how hard it was to get anything so glorious to grow in the chilly climes of the north-east. And then, once we got onto football and his beloved Town and Toon, well, he didn't stop. That was the wonderful thing about the man. You listened, you lapped it up, you felt like an old friend. No wonder producing that documentary about his life proved so emotional. He was one of a kind, the like of which we'll never see again.

Getting access to Sir Cliff Richard when he performed at a stately home in Norfolk involved endless waiting and jumping through hoops but, once there, he too was so generous with his time. Others included Sir Bobby Charlton, the enigmatic Brian Wilson from The Beach Boys, Dionne Warwick, Status Quo, Jamie Cullum, Brian Blessed, Alan Titchmarsh - who self-deprecatingly joked about people calling him Tit-marsh - Michael Aspel, Joe Pasquale, Steve Harley, John Alderton, Griff Rhys-Jones, Letitia Dean (Sharon Watts in Eastenders), the dancer Wayne Sleep, who was an absolute joy; numerous football managers at Ipswich Town, including John Duncan, John Lyall, George Burley, Joe Royle, Jim Magilton, Roy Keane, Paul Jewell and Mick McCarthy, and players like Mick Mills, Kevin Beattie, Terry Butcher and FA Cup hero Roger Osborne, one of the humblest men you'll ever meet.

Other luminaries who spring to mind include Sir Richard Branson, on board his record-breaking *Virgin Challenger II* in Lowestoft in 1986, Sir Ian Botham, Paula Radcliffe, when she was pounding the track in Bedford and whistling past me like the wind, even before she was really famous, the sailor Ellen MacArthur, who found it amusing that I was kitted out (on BBC instructions) in full life-saving kit, despite the fact that it was low tide at the boatyard in Ipswich where the interview took

The humble hero of Town's FA Cup win in '78, Roger Osborne

place, with no water, just mud all around us! Chris Packham, Michaela Strachan (both always a joy to be with), the snooker player Ray Reardon, the aforementioned Steve Harley from Cockney Rebel, who was always great company, and the jockey Frankie Dettori, who was polite, despite me interrupting his round of golf.

Talking of horse racing, there was also the late and great Julian Wilson. I had to interview him for a story at Newmarket, but I knew I'd have my hands full doing another chat elsewhere on the racecourse at around the same time. So, I enlisted the help of my wife Sally, who'd come out with me for the day. The only problem was that she didn't know Julian Wilson from Adam, so I gave her a rough description - pointed features, trilby, green/grey raincoat, that kind of look - and told her to stand by the weighing room, as that was where we'd agreed to meet, and to hold on to him until I ran over.

My other interview complete, I scuttled across to see the reassuring sight of Sally standing with someone, dressed in trilby and grey/green raincoat. It was only when the "guest" turned that I realised it wasn't Julian Wilson at all, but a rather bemused race-goer, who obviously hadn't wanted to offend anyone by admitting that he didn't actually know why he'd been collared. After profuse apologies, we all scanned around us and, thankfully, there was the real Julian Wilson! Relief all round. Interview done. No one any the wiser!

I also filmed twice with Nick Knowles from DIY SOS. On the first occasion, he was filming at Hullbridge in Essex and, when we turned up, he was adamant that we needed to appear in that episode of the programme and be a part of the story. That story involved him getting hit (pretend comedy style) on the back of the head with a builder's shovel. It was fun, and funny! The second time we met was in Mildenhall in 2017, when the team adapted the home of Simon Dobbin, a passionate football fan, who was left with brain damage and subsequently died, after being attacked following a match. It was a hugely emotional project anyway, but extra special for Nick, as this was the place where he lived and went to school. After arriving on site, meeting Nick and saying our hellos for the second time, the distinctive sight and sound of fellow presenter Laurence Llewelyn-Bowen caught our attention as he strode across the estate towards us, his long leather coat flowing behind him,

Nick Knowles, Laurence Llewelyn-Bowen and me in Mildenhall in 2017

shades on, hard-hat tipped at a jaunty angle. It was like a scene from *The Matrix*! Nick, Laurence and everyone else on site at the time were a joy to be around. The picture taken of the three of us remains an all-time favourite. The epitome of that saying about nice to be important, but more important to be nice.

But if fame is judged on absolute star quality and the ability to make, not just an entrance, but a room fall silent when you do, just one name comes to mind - Dame Joan Collins.

It involved a day out in London in February 2002 and, specifically, the London Palladium, where Dame Joan would be holding court during a press launch to celebrate the fact that, at the age of 69, she was returning to the stage and off on tour around the country in the romantic comedy *Full Circle*. Some of the shows would be in our patch, and so we joined a queue of other reporters and camera crews gathered for what would feel more like a speed-dating moment, as the star swept swiftly between tables, with everyone promised their own slot.

We made our way inside, across the polished floor and up the majestic staircase towards the glittering Val Parnell Bar, with its columns, beautifully ornate raised plasterwork and sparkling chandeliers. From memory, I think we had a ten-minute window, and we were all warned that we had to be ready to go without any hold-ups. This well-cho-reographed media call would wait for no one. I've witnessed plenty of bunfights, with sharp-elbowed, ill-tempered jostling, but this was almost military in its discipline and precision, aided by what felt like a phalanx of PR people and PAs, desperate to see things run smoothly. We all had our place; all had our deadlines to hit.

A bit like when a roadie appears on stage before the main act, to add that extra, yet critical piece of gaffer-tape, Dame Joan's husband, Percy Gibson, entered the room, casting what felt like a caring, cautious eye around the room, to make sure everything was set and then, in she glided, hair and make-up, as you'd expect, faultless. She was wearing a matching jacket and skirt of red leather, a white top, and pearl necklace. Suddenly, this was very real, very tense, as I tried in my head to rehearse my questions once more. Time would be tight; it would be pointless wasting precious seconds asking the same things that had already been posed by other reporters in the room, so I tried to loiter and listen, silently, surreptitiously. Professional etiquette dictates that you never compromise someone else's shot or sound recording. But it was a chance to establish what their line had been. What ground had they covered? What seemed to work well? Come on, Kev, blind her with your brilliance. Do I tell her she looks fabulous? No! I bet everyone tries that tack. Sycophantic. Sickly. Steer clear. Keep it simple. She's going back on stage, why? What was it about this production which appealed? That would kick things off. Blindingly original? Not really, but it'd do as a warm-up and she's no doubt keen to sell it as a must-see for the regional theatre-goers.

The camera operator, John Nichols, had the seating, lighting and radio mics set. I glanced across at Dame Joan. She seemed chilled, flicking her hair back just in case it needed a tweak. It didn't. And all the while she was edging closer.

Suddenly, this was it. She was upon me. I can't remember what I said. Probably, "Joan, you look fabulous!" but, in truth, it was a blur. Just look her right in the eyes, I'd told myself beforehand. So I did, and she looked right back, smiled the most enchanting smile and stroked her chin. Was that kind of body language good? A nod to say we were rolling from John who, frankly, had done all the work up to this point, and we were away.

Looking fabulous - Dame Joan Collins in 2002. Picture: BBC

"I think it's extremely entertaining. Very funny and I think it's an audience-pleaser," she told me. "I hope, I hope, I hope the audiences are going to like it." She added with extra emphasis.

"Cos essentially," I replied, "You're the kind of person who likes to make people laugh?"

"Yes, I do. Did you ever see my *Cinzano* commercials?"

Of course, those ads with Leonard Rossiter; who could ever doubt her skill at comic - timing? Frankly, she had done pretty much everything since making her stage debut at the age of nine.

Now, on the verge of 70, why do it? Why commit to some 14 weeks of touring around the country, and how long did she want to carry on?

"As long as I can," came the response, fast and fiery. "What's the point of quitting? What am I gonna do - sit and knit? I can't knit! I don't want to sit and eat buns and watch TV."

"Everything I read about you still says sexy, glamorous. How do you do it?"

Joan pondered for a moment and then, in a flash, the seasoned pro kicked in. "Well, you'll have to read my book _ out now in paperback _ £9.99 - Looking Good, Feeling Great - by Joan Collins!" As for the more considered response, it was, she told me, all about good luck, good genes and discipline and, as she flashed that trademark smile, who would argue?

Some celebrities disappoint - not this one! Picture: BBC

In no time at all, we'd reached the end of our allotted time, so we said our thank-yous and then she glided away to the next waiting lens. The essence of style and showbiz. A fleeting moment, but what a moment. She wouldn't remember me, but I'd remember Dame Joan. Thank you. It made my day!

"The secret of having a personal life is not answering too many questions about it."

Dame Joan Collins

Chapter Thirteen

The Horse's Mouth

People always accuse journalists of being interested only in bad news. But, if I look back over my career, I've probably spent more time reporting the heart-warming, funny, odd and quirky. TV is all about light and shade, rise and fall, contrast, and I always felt that those lighter moments were essential, not just for the feel of our output, but for the audience. I always had a thought in my head which I was told, very early on, about what viewers want from us and it's, "Take me somewhere and show me something - something I wouldn't normally get to see."

We genuinely were their eyes and ears. The fact that I was invariably having a ball doing it probably added to their sense of joy. I hope it did, anyway.

One day sticks in my mind. I had a call from a local pub and a couple - Steve and Julie - whose own story was compelling. Both made redundant from their jobs at a local factory, they were at a loss, initially, to know what to do next. But they decided to take on the pub and take their chances. However, there was a twist in the tale, because the other thing which they had, as well as bag-loads of drive and passion, was an old fire engine called Freddie, a beautifully-restored 1955 Bedford. Julie spotted it online and they jumped at the chance. Steve even had the uniform to match.

So what's a reporter to do, when offered the chance to ride shotgun, and ring the brass bell in this marauding monster of a motor vehicle? We set off down winding country lanes, with a drone filming us too from on high, and Steve warning me that he'd need a fair bit of time to brake. He did, but thankfully we always had enough time to stop when we encountered other drivers, especially once we hit the downhill run.

And it was odd that here we were, trundling through the countryside, ringing the bell, and making hell and all racket, yet everyone we passed didn't bat an eyelid. Just the customary polite wave. It was obviously the kind of thing I imagine they expected in Suffolk, in the middle of nowhere, on a sunny afternoon. It was a classic example of that old journalistic saying that everyone has a story to tell. They do, and thank goodness for that. The film went out. I'd had the best day. I think Steve and Julie had, too. They've invited me back for another road trip, ringing that bell. I will most definitely accept!

One other story where I probably displayed a little too much enthusiasm was about a circus coming to town. I wanted to make it look a bit different, and I knew that one of the acts we'd be filming was an artiste who could bend her body into the most unlikely positions. So, on the morning of the story, I contacted Coes, a long-established department store just around the corner from the BBC's office in Ipswich, to ask if they had a mannequin we could borrow. In no time at all, they'd found a spare and I went to collect it. That's the other thing about TV - people will always go to great lengths, often at the drop of a hat, to help you out.

I popped the mannequin in the car, collected a spare pair of trousers from home, and headed to the circus, where I met Les, who would be on the camera. I explained what I had in mind, and he, too, I think, saw the comedy potential.

In the car I changed into my spare trousers, and put the ones I'd been wearing on to the mannequin, along with my shoes, and we then proceeded to film a sequence of the performer doing this incredible thing where she brought her legs over the back of her head so her feet sat flat on the ground either side of her face. I then moved into her slot and, with the mannequin's legs carefully positioned, created the illusion of me doing exactly the same trick. I think I added a corny line about it looking tough but, actually, once you try, there's really nothing to it. Thankfully, it raised a giggle, but I'm not sure reporters would try it now. Too slapstick.

Royalty, too, can be funny. I remember covering a story in Mistley on the Essex-Suffolk border, when Prince Charles was being shown around an old maltings building which had been converted into homes. It was one of those days when everything smelled of fresh paint! Spotlessly clean, ready for the VIP.

We knew that the Prince would be going inside one of the homes to meet its owners, and we'd be doing our usual bit afterwards, once he'd moved out, popping in to say hello and ask them how it went. Were you nervous? Did you make him a cup of tea? That kind of predictable, banal stuff.

The problem, though, was that space was tight and so, as the Prince made his way up the stairs, I couldn't easily get out of his way and I had, nestling in my arms, the large microphone which I'd often carry for the crew between interviews, complete with its grey, furry covering, designed to prevent any wind from distorting and ruining the sound. It had a resemblance to a cross between a small dog and a badger, and was so often a source of amusement.

The Prince drew close and, spotting the furry thing, asked if I was going to be holding it all day and remarking that it did, indeed, look like a dog. He giggled - we all did. He then went inside, did his stuff, and then, when he emerged, instantly broke into the widest of smiles again and said, "Ooh, look, he's still got it!"

A short while later, we moved on through the building and into a room where the Prince was about to say a few words. As he was waiting to be formally introduced, he looked across and we made eye contact. He gave me the warmest of smiles. It was just lovely, and all because of a bundle of fur!

People are incredibly generous. I've lost count of the times I've had total strangers emerge from their homes when I've been working outside, either filming or editing in the car, to offer me tea or coffee. Moments like that always blew me away. They had no need to do it, but they just wanted to show me kindness. That sort of generosity was something I never took for granted.

Someone else who left his mark was the aforementioned actor, Brian Blessed. It was 2005, and he was coming to Ipswich and the Regent Theatre for panto, to play Captain Hook. To help promote the show, he was heading out into the Wet Dock in Ipswich on an old barge. We were going with him. It would prove one of the funniest days.

Brian isn't just loud, he's a force of nature. Les was again on camera, and the first thing Brian told him was to "keep the lens where the money is, Les!" We thought it would be funny for Brian, who was in full costume, to emerge in a fury through the hatch on deck, waving his sword around. Well, he wasn't just up for it, he attacked it with gusto; so much so that he launched into the wrong, but still pirate-related, piece of dialogue. We went again. This time, it was the genuine Captain Hook, and hilarious; in fact, we had to tell Brian, politely at that early stage, that we already had more than enough. I think he would've happily carried on performing on deck until darkness fell, giving us enough footage to fill the entire edition of Look East that night.

But what was most impressive was that on board were some youngsters; I can't recall precisely why, but I think they might have been sea cadets, to add to the backdrop, and Brian spent a long time talking to them about life, about aspiration and rising to a challenge. This was a man who'd climbed mountains, including Everest, trekked to the North Pole, explored jungles; in short, a true adventurer and here urging these teenagers to reach for the stars. It was some moment. I subsequently saw the panto at the theatre, and it was one of the funniest I've ever watched. Blessed has this remarkable energy, this wonderful ability to switch in an instant from mirth to menace and, when things went wrong on stage, as they always do, he wallowed in the moment. A great, booming presence, but, behind the scenes, what a man!

Another person it was always a joy to be around was John Fleming, who's devoted so much of his life to the majestic, yet threatened, Suffolk Horse. He's respected for his knowledge and experience as a breeder, yet is the most gentle and unassuming of men. Always happy to make time for filming, whenever the Suffolk and its fight for survival were in the news.

I always remember being at the Suffolk Show one year and asking someone who was showing them what qualities you needed. The answer? The ability to move quickly!

The wonderful John Fleming, who's devoted his life to the Suffolk Horse

They might be gentle, but they're huge and can weigh up to a tonne. John always reminded me of that old saying about a Suffolk having the face of an angel - and a backside like a farmer's daughter!

I was filming John with some of his animals at Ufford and he'd told me, in passing, when I mentioned their gentle nature, that they were like children and needed to be told firmly who's boss. Interview complete, John left me by the field, as I had to get a few extra shots and I needed to do the obligatory piece to camera. I was, as I so often did, self-shooting and filming myself with my own camera, which I'd set up on the tripod, so that the shot was nicely framed, exposed and focused. I then stepped back just a foot or so to stand by the metal gate. My plan was to be gently stroking the muzzle of one of John's mares, who was clearly highly inquisitive.

I delivered the words for about the third time, just to make sure it was OK, when the horse suddenly went from a gentle nibble and clamped her gums onto my index finger. It was, quite frankly, bloody excruciating and, while I was determined to get to the end of the sentence, I realised that she wasn't going to let go and I thought it might get even worse

80

if I tried to tug it free. She finally relented after I pleaded, "Get off, ya bugger!" Bugger being a traditional Suffolk expletive, which she clearly understood. My finger was left looking angry and bruised. So much so, that I was told by my producer to fill in an injury report form for BBC safety. Imagine how that read? Bitten, or rather "gummed", on location by a big horse. John was right. They need to know who's boss!

In fact, it's true what they say about working with children and animals. Both rarely sit still and do what you want them to, on cue, in front of camera. But then television can be an incredibly boring, drawn-out process, with take after take, so who could blame them? On the rare occasions when it did all work out, they were the undoubted stars, time and time again!

Birds, too, could be a source of rich entertainment. I remember going to an estate in Ipswich to interview a young woman, who was fiercely protective of pigeons. As I recall, it was all to do with a story about them possibly being culled at the town's port, where they'd become - as pigeons do - something of a pest. In fact, she was so

fascinated by them that she kept one as a pet. It was incredibly intelligent and, when we'd finished out interview, she asked me if I would like it to sit on my head. Clarifying that I'd heard her correctly and she'd said "sit on my head", I obliged, and it was actually quite a cute thing and didn't disgrace itself at all. In fact, a real journalistic coo! Get in!

We frequently spent time trying to track down missing birds. The audience (and producers!) always seemed to love the thrill of the chase when a huge bird of prey escaped and was on the loose. One

Another bird-brained moment! 2018 such avian adventure took us to

Leiston, on the off-chance that we might spot an Eagle Owl, which had slipped out from its enclosure.

The truth, of course, was that this bird - who I think was called Dawn - could be sat on a branch virtually anywhere and impossible to spot, unless it took flight right near us, when its wingspan of close on two metres would be hard to miss.

Jamie Niblock was with me on the camera, and we spent pretty much most of the morning prowling in vain. The bird's owner believed that, unless she was really hungry, she'd probably be sitting tight in the trees - possibly for some days.

We spoke to a few people living nearby, but they'd seen nothing, even with the aid of binoculars.

So, with time to spare and little to do but wait, Jamie and I went for a wander in the woods, and it was on the way that he revealed his wide knowledge about birds from when he used to keep them as a youngster. Not just that, but he also had an uncanny knack of doing bird impressions.

In a flash, he cupped both hands to his mouth and made the most incredibly realistic sound of an owl hooting. It was so real that I feared that, at any moment, this elusive Eagle Owl might swoop down on us from on high, in the false belief that it'd found a mate. It didn't.

I obviously wasn't the only person who was impressed, though, because, when we emerged from the bushes, we bumped into a chap walking his dog, and who recognised my face and asked - not unexpectedly - what we were up to. When we told him we were hoping to film a missing owl, he suggested, "You'd do well to try over there, 'cos I'm sure I just heard one!" So, it remains a mystery to this day. Did he actually hear an owl, or was it Jamie? I think we both knew the answer!

Chapter Fourteen

Seeing the World

I mentioned earlier how my first day at the BBC was spent on the picket line, protesting about cuts, and that need to tighten the shoe-strings has been a constant during my time with the Corporation. In both local radio and regional television, budgets were always under pressure, and it was funny how the public perceived what we were up to. I remember turning up for one filming job and, once I'd parked my leased and modest Peugeot on the driveway at the interviewee's home, he told me he thought I'd have something like a Jag, given the money I was on! Little did he know.

For a good part of my time filming with BBC Look East, as I mentioned, I worked as a video journalist, which meant that it was just me doing the reporting, the filming and the editing. Billy-no-mates, whipping around like a blue-arsed fly getting all the facts, all the clips, or the angles. Don't get me wrong, I loved it, but it was tough work, so it always made me smile when contributors would frequently tell me upon my arrival, "Is that it? Just you? I was expecting a few more people!" The beauty was that, while it was pressured, you had control, you knew what you wanted to shoot, knew what the edit would need, so it felt a very economical, efficient way to operate and rarely, if ever, did anyone complain at the finished piece. In fact, they'd invariably speak of their amazement that it all came together looking so smooth and accomplished.

Occasionally, though, the BBC would allow you to argue the case for one-offs, if the story justified it and, more to the point, justified the expense. Key to that was ensuring that whatever it produced would run across all platforms in the BBC - TV, radio, digital - the whole shooting-match. So, I felt blessed to have been deployed abroad three times with the BBC. I'm not sure they would get the nod today!

The first was in 2001 - a trip to the deserts in the Gulf state of Oman, to film a huge military exercise called *Operation Swift Sword II*. It cost some £93 million, lasted about six weeks and involved, it was estimated, a quarter of the UK's armed forces, making it our largest deployment since the 1991 Gulf War. An invasion of Oman by a small, fictional country, intent on seizing control of its oilfields, was the scenario and it was designed to show, said the Defence Secretary at the time, "Britain's ability to deploy rapidly, a considerable force with real punch over strategic distances."

But on a wider canvas, the timing was everything because, while things had been planned long before, it was actually taking place amid rising tensions in the region, shortly after the 9/11 attacks in America.

Camera operator Nick Waterworth and myself were called up to do it at relatively short notice, because we'd both undertaken hostile environment training and the BBC rating for this zone had just gone up several notches, making that training an essential requirement.

It was a long flight out. As I recall, made even longer because we had to fly around the airspace of Iraq, but we arrived at the airport in Muscat, the capital of Oman, and stepped outside to be met by our hosts from the RAF, into what I can only describe as searing heat.

We would be staying at the InterContinental Hotel, and strolling into the vast, opulent and delightfully air-conditioned atrium which served as reception, it gave us, in hindsight, exactly the wrong idea about what this trip would be like.

In no time at all, we were off in a minibus to an area of Seeb airfield, where the military had already established a base. Arriving at the perimeter entrance, it was clear to see that things were edgy. An Omani guard poked the end of his rifle through one of the small windows, unsure who we were, or why we were there. Our RAF minders quickly ensured calm but, as we went to move on, none of the men standing by the main gate was prepared to open it. The reason? The driver of the vehicle was female.

Reporting from Oman in 2001. Picture: BBC

Once inside, we finally set up to start filming and it felt as if, every few seconds, an aircraft - mostly heavyweights like the Hercules - was landing or taking-off. Noise and swirling sand all around. Omani security guards regularly patrolling past us in their green-and-khaki-coloured camouflaged vehicles, machine guns pointing front and rear.

Twenty thousand men and women from the UK were out here, including helicopter crews from Wattisham in Suffolk, Tornado crews from RAF Marham in Norfolk, and bomb disposal teams from RAF Wittering in Cambridgeshire. They, and others also based in our region, would clearly be the focus of our report.

We popped into the one area which is always a hive of activity - the mess. The temperature inside was 65 degrees Celsius. It was, I would note in the first of the three reports we would produce, the one place where you needed to step outside to cool down. And, if you did step outside, on a noticeboard, cuttings from papers back home. They, too, gave a sense of the mood. "Blair turns up the heat on the Taliban," said one.

While Seeb was home to the big planes, the airfield at Thumrait in southern Oman was where the fast jets and most of the troops were based, and it was there we were heading next, in a Hercules. Once on board, we were given a series of instructions by the loadmaster, one of which was that, if we were forced to make an emergency landing, we were to use the exit door at the front and turn right, not left. The propellers were on the left!

We were also told not to film anything while on board, because there were individuals here who mustn't be identified. That prompted me to start scanning around the fuselage, only to avert my eyes pretty quickly when they locked on to one fellow-passenger, who you could tell was part of that "special" breed and was clearly trying hard to lie low. He returned my look with an icy stare.

The funny thing about a Hercules is that your seat is made from webbing, and you're facing inwards, with no windows, so you have no awareness of what's happening, which explains why the RAF press liaison officer sitting next to me seemed surprised when I remarked on the smooth take-off. He explained that the runway was an extremely long one, and we were still rumbling along it, yet to get airborne!

We arrived in Thumrait after a two-hour flight to see the most beautiful sunset as darkness fell. A key instruction as we went to leave the plane was not to film anything in certain parts of the airfield. The Americans maintained the ability to use Omani bases through what's called the Oman Facilities Access Agreement. It was clear that they'd been slowly building-up huge military assets on base, and were obviously keen to keep that little secret under their berets for now.

Frankly, I was knackered, so delighted to be shown to our sleeping accommodation. A tent in the desert. One among hundreds which had been erected. The scale of it was breath-taking. Row upon row and, even now, late in the evening, the heat never seemed to relent, nor the noise. Jets screamed in the skies overhead. A moment to feel pretty insignificant in the grand scheme of things.

We'd been warned about the dangers here. Not just the searing heat, but also sandstorms, spiders and scorpions. I decided to sleep with my desert boots on. Seemed wise. The camp bed was basic, but off I drifted in no time at all, like a baby.

Next morning, I woke early to find that Nick had already disappeared. He was out capturing the sunrise. He knew how quick you had to be to shoot that moment, and it ensured that the films we'd produce had, within them, some of the most beautiful images I'd ever seen.

Ready to go in Oman. Picture: BBC

We quickly got our bearings. How to work the water supply in the showers, which were primitive, but perfectly OK. Toilets and wash basins, too, were plentiful. A reminder that hygiene in a place like this, where everyone needs to remain fit and healthy, was key.

We gathered sequences and interviews around the site, saw fighter pilots honing their skills on the bombing ranges, helicopter crews shuttling around, with a string of camels in the desert below, it was just something else, and everyone was keen to be involved, keen to ensure that their families back home saw what this deployment entailed.

A member of one of the fighter crews even sidled up to us at one point to ask if we wanted some in-flight cockpit footage he'd shot himself - as long as we didn't show any of the equipment on board - of a low pass at speed through the jagged and stunning desert terrain. Of course, we said yes! The shots would be the icing on the cake for the final film.

The food on base was plentiful and superb. Even when we arrived at the mess to find that the evening's offering was a red-hot curry, we all piled in. The first time that I've sat eating a meal with sweat pouring down my face and my shirt drenched through!

Alcohol, though, was more complicated. When we arrived, it transpired that there'd been some shenanigans. A few people had taken advantage of the "two cans a day" rule on site, so the top brass had introduced a ban. It was lifted, eventually, before we left, but, personally,

I didn't mind. The essential liquid here was water. Stacks and stacks of it piled high at every corner, and we were encouraged to keep on drinking. Dehydration another danger. No wonder they were getting through around a million litres of water a day!

Filming done, we flew back north to Muscat and the elegant and exquisite surroundings of the InterContinental Hotel. Talk about extremes, and I dread to think how the other residents must have felt as this small band of dirty, sandy and sweat-stained journos piled through the doors! But, after a shower, it was down to the bar, where we ordered beer, standing alongside Omani men wearing traditional white robes, getting their own fill of Foster's lager. A land of contrasts and a trip to remember. Needless to say, after several days parched in the heat, we all got squiffy pretty rapidly!

Trip number two came a year later, with a visit to the United States to witness the celebrations to mark 400 years since Suffolk explorer Bartholomew Gosnold - an enthusiastic promoter of colonisation - sailed across the Atlantic in his 39-foot-long ship, *Concord*, to what would become New England. It was Gosnold, born in 1571 at Otley, who gave Cape Cod its name, for its abundant fish, and also Martha's Vineyard, in memory of his young daughter who died. He also built a fort on one of the islands there - known today as Cuttyhunk.

I'd be making the trip with camera operator Shaun Whitmore and, having suggested the idea and the need for us to be there to see the moment at first hand, it was down to me to plan it and cost it! Flights across the Atlantic, hotels, car bookings, even the seaplane we'd need to organise to fly us over to Cuttyhunk, where festivities were planned around the memorial - a stone tower - erected on the island in his memory.

It got the thumbs-up, and so Shaun and I flew out to Boston and then drove, in a hire vehicle, south - stopping off at various places to gather shots of some of the towns and villages which bear the names of the places in the East of England from where those pioneers originated. Ipswich, Holbrook, Framlingham, Sudbury, Haverhill and so many more.

Thankfully, everything went smoothly and according to plan and, even when we pitched up at what felt like an airfield in the middle of nowhere, the pilot who would fly us out to Cuttyhunk was duly waiting to meet us.

He was incredibly chilled. Almost to a worrying degree, telling us about the short flight out there being a doddle. The only fly in the ointment was if you forgot to change the wheels to the floats, which were, after all, pretty essential for a smooth landing in the bay. He'd been caught out quite recently, he told us, as he loaded our camera kit on board, resulting in the plane pitching rather sharply forward on landing and scaring the life out of the occupants!

I'd had a taste of this nonchalant demeanour when I was making the booking on the phone some weeks before. The BBC, quite rightly, needed a lot of hurdles cleared in terms of safety. Things like the airworthiness of the plane, the pilot's competence, insurance papers. I think he thought that simply telling me that he'd done this trip hundreds of times would be enough. It wasn't, but eventually he faxed over the documents we needed to see, albeit somewhat reluctantly.

Anyway, there we were, on the runway, engine running, talking to the local control tower, and ready for the off. It was cosy. I was sitting with the pilot, Shaun was in the back, nursing his camera. In no time at all, we were in the air and climbing. It was the most glorious day, but we hadn't reckoned on the heat and humidity. It was baking on board and, within minutes, the look on Shaun's face changed. The camera had overheated and was unresponsive. Below us, the most magnificent views of a crystal-blue sea and ahead, in the distance, Cuttyhunk island itself. The bay circled by verdant hills, with dazzling white, sandy beaches. It was stunning, but we couldn't shoot a frame. Even holding open the small vents to let the air rush through, did little to ease the stifling heat.

During the flight, the pilot asked me, very matter-of-factly to, "pull that lever." Knowing that to tamper inadvertently with some vital piece of equipment might spell trouble, I double-checked that I'd grasped the right one and then pulled. I didn't know until a little while later that the lever in question was the slightly essential wheels-or-floats control. It obviously all went OK because, after a fairly steep descent, we touched down as light as a feather onto the water and then chugged our away towards one of the wooden pontoons.

It was like a scene from *Jaws*. Dozens of fishing boats of varying sizes, with wooden lobster-huts and lobster pots all around. But what caught my eye more than anything was the sight of someone waving at me from the pontoon. It was my dear friend, David Webb, and his wife, Jean. David had come out, too, to cover the celebrations for radio. He opted for the ferry, so I knew that they'd be here at some point, but how joyous to have a welcoming committee on hand!

Talking of welcomes, the generosity and kindness of the local people was overwhelming. Much of that was down to the timing. It was the Fourth of July. Independence Day. The place was alive with colour, bunting and flags and they greeted us with such warmth, keen to help us understand and delve deep into the Gosnold story. This island, home to around 50 people, was originally called Poocuohhunkkunnah, but renamed "Elizabeth's Isle" by the explorer when he arrived at what was to become New England in his ship in 1602, intent on creating a new colony.

It was remarkably moving to retrace the footsteps. One of the locals dressed up in costume to play the part of Gosnold, and we marched in procession to gather for a special service near the 70-foot stone memorial, built in 1902.

A truly poignant moment. The perfect setting. The perfect day.

We had a flight to catch to return to the mainland, but one couple wouldn't let us leave without inviting us to their island home, with views to die for, and there we sat, on rocking-chairs, savouring - for the first time - a root beer. It was idyllic, and the fact that the filming had gone like a dream and we knew we'd captured some stunning pictures, made the drink taste even sweeter!

Thankfully, it was less humid on the return flight in the seaplane, the camera was OK and so Shaun finally captured those wonderful images from on high.

Back in Boston, we had more treats in store. We managed to get media passes for what's called The Boston Pops, a festival of live music for Independence Day and, topping the bill, Barry Manilow - to be

Cuttyhunk, USA, 2002. Picture: Shaun Whitmore

followed by fireworks. As Shaun and I made our way there, having stopped to admire the, for me, legendary *Cheers!* bar from the TV comedy series, we found ourselves part of a heaving swarm of people. Thousands of concert-goers were heading in, too but, in the midst of it all, I looked up and who should be there? David Webb and Jean again. What were the chances of that? And were they stalking me, or were we stalking them?!

Inside the venue, we were guided to a special raised area, set aside for the media crews, and watched as Manilow ran through hit after hit. In fact, pretty much every one of his classic songs. It was pinch yourself time. Hard to believe we were part of this most special of moments, and feeling slightly guilty, as the national anthem was played and we stood rather awkwardly, unsure of the right words, unsure of the right demeanour, as the spectators around us sang their hearts out in a rousing chorus, most with hands on hearts, some in tears. Few do patriotism better than the Americans!

The fireworks followed. A truly breathtaking display and, at the heart of it all, with the sky awash with explosive colour, Shaun and I filmed a piece to camera, with me pondering what Gosnold himself would've made of this moment. Trying to get my words to dovetail neatly with the whizzes and bangs was an achievement in itself!

The third trip was to Anzio, and what would prove a truly emotional few days, involving a man called Walter Nixon, who returned to southern Italy in May 2019 for the first time since he served there 75 years ago.

Walter, who was 96 at the time, was a wireless operator who took part in an amphibious landing behind German lines in January 1944 during the Battle of Anzio, which involved some of the toughest fighting seen during the entire Second World War. Horrendous conditions, with heavy casualties.

And he'd never returned; he didn't even have a passport but, finally, he got one and, accompanied by his son Keith and his grandson Paul, he went back to visit the graves of some of the thousands who died.

Shoot-edit camera operator John Fairhall and I arrived in the evening and, having met the family at the hotel, went with them the next morning as Walter paid his respects during the first of two visits

he would make to cemeteries there with us alongside him. It was profoundly moving, as a lifetime of raw emotion welled to the surface. Walter in tears, remembering the loss of so many, so young, raging about the futility of war.

I didn't really need to ask questions. Walter just told it like it was. The words flowed. Unstoppable and unimaginable. Painful and poignant.

The following day, it was the Beach Head War Cemetery and, in a moment made even more

Walter Nixon at Anzio 2019   atmospheric by the sound of a relentless downpour, Walter was again overcome, as he finally located the grave of a Captain West, the man he'd helped pull from a trench when a bomb went off right beside them. He couldn't be saved. All those years ago, but now this most precious of moments, a comrade winding back the clock and standing tall to salute, the raindrops falling non-stop from the front of his regimental beret. The words, We Will Remember Them, and the haunting sound of The Last Post being played took on a whole new meaning after those sobering scenes. One man's memories. One man's pilgrimage. One man's humbling show of respect.

It was telling that, when John and I went back to our hotel room and, late that night, over a few beers and a bottle of red wine, started to edit the first of the films we'd produce for Look East from Anzio, we replayed that sequence of Walter in the cemetery getting so upset time and again, as you do when you're refining the cut on the laptop. And no matter how often we watched it through, it choked us up every single time. It was real, it was remarkable, and it was raw - unflinchingly so.

There were, though, lighter moments, too. Walter remembering, with still ill-disguised frustration, the senior officer who took the best biscuits from his tin, and offered inferior ones in return. And looking

Walter Nixon finally back at the beach

down over the beach itself, Walter recalled how he was one of the first to come ashore and had driven his vehicle across the sand, desperately seeking shelter and safety. As he did so, someone yelled at him. "Come on, come on, come on! Don't stop!" was the cry. "All right mate!" was Walter's measured response. The "mate" in question turned out to be Denis Healey! Remarkably, the pair would meet again years later when Healey, then a Labour MP, came to make a speech in Ipswich and joined Walter, a lifelong trade unionist and socialist, on the campaign trail.

One thing Walter had been keen to do on his return was to take back some sand as a memento. A reminder of everything that happened - everything he saw. But the long flight of steps down to the sea made that impossible so, while his son and grandson made the descent instead on his behalf, we remained up top, chatting like old friends. He made me think. He made me giggle. He'd made it back. Finally, after all those years. Lest we forget.

Anzio 2019

Chapter Fifteen

Beyond Words

This chapter was the one about which I hesitated the most. I couldn't not include the awful events of 2006 and how five women died at the hands of serial killer Steve Wright. But, at the same time, it was so painful for so many that I felt a real sense of trepidation trying to recount the story.

It was covered at the time, and has been re-told since, in such minute detail, that I don't seek to re-tell it again; but what I will try to do, succinctly, is to say how it felt as a journalist. A local journalist. Covering a story on the doorstep, which grew so fast into something which none of us, at the very beginning, could ever have imagined.

On 7th November 2006, police said that they were extremely concerned about Tania Nicol, who was 19 and had gone missing after leaving her home in Ipswich a few days before. Her mother Kerry said it was odd for her not to be in touch with her family.

Eight days later, police made a further appeal for information, this time about Gemma Adams, who was 25 and had been reported missing by her partner in Ipswich. We filmed posters going up, asking for help to try to find her.

I think there was an assumption that they'd turn up eventually and, as journalists, we always treated any disappearance with a great deal of care in the early stages, for exactly that reason.

The charity Missing People says that 176,000 people go missing in the UK every year, and someone's reported missing every 90 seconds. Most are experiencing some kind of vulnerability or risk. 75% of adults who disappear are found within 24 hours.

But of Tania and Gemma, despite repeated police appeals, there was no sign. Then, on Saturday, 2nd December, a body was found in a brook at Hintlesham. The following day it was identified as being that of Gemma, and detectives launched a major inquiry, speaking of their fears for Tania too, given that both women were from the same area and there were obvious similarities.

On the Monday, I was sent to the spot where the body had been found, as specialist teams started searching the area for any clues as to what, precisely, had happened. It was, as I recall, a damp, grim winter's day, as we stood waiting, in the car park of a local fishery just off the main road between Ipswich and Hadleigh, for the lead detective to appear and be interviewed. I always ran through beforehand the areas that we'd like to cover. It was a sensible way to ensure there was common understanding of the kind of questions I'd be asking. But, in all honesty, there was, at a moment like this, only so far you could go. There were inevitably, still, so many unknowns, so we talked about the specific details of where the body was found and by whom, and what the police might want from the wider public, in terms of seeing or hearing anything suspicious. A parked car, an individual, anything which might form part of the jigsaw.

But this was an investigation which would gather pace at a frightening rate and, just four days later, another body was found in the same stretch of water, two miles away, near Copdock Mill. Confirmation that it was Tania came the next day and then, the day after that, a third body was found in woodland at Nacton.

The discovery had been made just after 3pm and, later that afternoon, I got a call from a source, telling me about intense police activity at the spot, which was just a mile from where we lived. I arrived, and pulled-up at the bus stop opposite the road leading down to the village of Nacton, which had been sealed off. It was an awful night, and I set up my camera and tripod to get a few shots of the scene and the large red "Road Closed" signs, in the cold, driving rain. The body had been found a short distance into the trees, just before the entrance to what was Amberfield School.

This was by now, of course, the only story that people were talking about, and the fact that this discovery had been made so close to home, looking back on it, had a profound impact. I well remember in the days that followed, as speculation grew that this was the work of a serial killer targeting women, how quickly the fear spread.

All three women who'd died had been sex-workers but, within the wider community, no one felt safe any more. The streets of Ipswich should've been awash with pre-Christmas shoppers and cheer, instead they were eerily quiet. I filmed at one restaurant, where the owner spoke of the steps they were taking to make sure their female staff made it safely home at night, after their shift finished. The police were urging women to stay together to stay safe, to keep away from any of the red-light areas and also promoting the offer of rape alarms on a stall at the town's market.

After the discovery of the third body at Nacton, the main road past the spot would be closed off for some weeks, leading to frustration for local traders who feared losing vital festive business.

But, if the community was worried now, things would intensify further the very next day, as detectives spoke of their concern for two more women who were missing - Paula Clennell, who was 24, and Annette Nicholls, 29.

The assistant chief constable warned prostitutes to stay off the streets for their own safety, but the police, the media, local people hardly had time to process one development before the case - which, by now was on the front page of almost every newspaper and leading every TV and radio bulletin morning and night - took another twist.

It was 12th December and what proved one of the most dramatic days. The routine was, as you'd expect, unpredictable, but the usual pattern was that on most days the police would call a news conference. These were normally held in the main hall of their headquarters at Martlesham, and so fast-moving was the inquiry that I can remember watching at times the senior detectives and their press team huddled in a corridor just of the main area, locked in last-minute discussions about what they now knew, and what information they planned to impart to the media, who were waiting with bated breath for the latest press release to be handed round.

By now, the media presence was huge. What could only be described as a mass of reporters, camera crews and photographers, all jostling for a space, all with editors back at base desperate for more, all with deadlines to hit.

It was at times chaotic as the camera crews, especially, desperately tried to secure a slot to ensure the best shot, but television dramas do us no favours when they portray the press pack as a menacing mob, surging forward, wildly out of control, to shout questions in the faces of senior officers. In reality, things were always pretty civilised. Invariably, the focus would fall on Detective Chief Superintendent Stewart Gull, sitting front and centre at the main table before us, a huge, silver constabulary crest behind him. He established himself very quickly as the calm, trusted face of the force, setting out what had changed … what they now knew ... what help they needed. After that, he'd take questions from around the room. A chance for some to check and clarify; a chance for others to go for glory, knowing that the cameras were on them, by lobbing in a leading or loaded question. But Mr Gull was too cute to reveal more than they needed, more than they wanted. Carefully controlling that flow of information was key.

So there we were on that critical day, waiting, as I recall, in the early afternoon for an update, having fed a fresh piece for our lunchtime bulletin. It was then that my colleague, Les, who was minutes away from the HQ, having filmed some other pictures close by, called to say that there was activity at nearby Levington. Roads were being closed and the police helicopter was circling an area not far from where the third body had already been found.

I was wary of making too much commotion, and thereby alerting everyone else, so I left as casually as I could, out to the car park and headed off, driving past the BT tower on my left and out towards Levington and what was the old A45. When I arrived and met Les, the stretch of road had already been sealed off, so again we filmed what we could of the police activity within the cordon. It was clear that this was again a significant crime-scene, and just how significant was quickly revealed. A member of the public had seen a body just metres from the road and the police helicopter, once at the scene and with a bird's-eye view, spotted a second one nearby. I can remember saying to myself, as we stood there with darkness falling, "It's now five." Five victims discovered in just 10 days. It's what criminologists call a spree, and this story had developed so quickly that it was hard to fathom the scale of what was unfolding before our eyes. I called the news desk. The sense of disbelief there, too, was clear.

A short while later, back in the hall, Stewart Gull confirmed the latest find and admitted that he feared the worst, in suspecting that this was Paula and Annette. That day, detectives also identified the third body found at Nacton as that of Anneli Alderton. She was 24 and had been expecting a baby.

And at that moment, we got a sense of what the force was trying to process, with the incident room handling, in just one day, more than two thousand calls. This was, by a country mile, the biggest inquiry it'd ever faced. The chief constable at the time, Alastair McWhirter, admitted that the magnitude of the inquiry - called Operation Sumac - meant they would have to rely on help, not just from neighbouring forces, but from those around the country. So, by 18th December, 650 officers were working on the case and, on the streets, police vehicles bearing the crests of Greater Manchester, Merseyside and others became a common sight.

The case was fast-moving, and so too was the process of news-gathering. Producers on the news desk were trying to second-guess what might happen next and frequently getting side-tracked by reports in the national press, which relied more on speculation than hard facts. My view, every morning, was that we had to see where the story would take us; and, every day, it did just that. Everybody was on alert and so, whenever there was police activity in Ipswich itself, or the surrounding area, it would be quickly noted and the media tipped off. But by now, of course, we were hunting with a very big pack, and so even if you pitched-up to the latest location of interest pretty promptly, you would soon be joined, first by a few other reporters and photographers, and then by the hordes. Personal reputation could help to a degree. If someone recognised you as a trusted face, it could mean a head start but, on most occasions, with the town as swamped as it was, potential interviewees had either already had enough, or would request money and insist that other outlets had already offered to pay, so why not us? I never did.

As well as what was happening day-to-day, the case triggered a much wider debate about the sex industry. About the reasons why it existed in the first place, the clients, the risks, the need for change. At least one MP urged ministers to press ahead with a plan to legalise small brothels. It would subsequently lead to a totally fresh approach in Ipswich, with a myriad of agencies and charities working together with the police and residents in a drive to support the women working on the streets, to get them out of prostitution and help them rebuild their lives. It was pioneering work, rightly hailed for the remarkable transformation it achieved.

The BBC had taken the view, very early on in the case, that the five victims were women first and prostitutes second and, as local reporters, we felt it incumbent upon us to take the utmost care in the way we spoke about them, and the tone throughout our coverage. It became clear to me, as I pursued various avenues, that in this town, my home town, you didn't need to look far before you found someone who knew one of the women or their families. They were all, as a fund-raising campaign would later acknowledge in its title, "somebody's daughter" and, to the frustration of many, their whole lives were being defined because of a choice made through desperation. It's reckoned that women who sell sex in this country are six times more likely to die - that's the highest for any group of women - and 18 times more likely to be murdered (*British Medical Journal*).

One of the most moving interviews I undertook in these dark days was with Jim Duell, Tania's father, who agreed to talk about his daughter, her life and her struggles. I went to his flat on the Chantry estate. He was the most humble, gentle of men, with a strong faith and, while we were chatting, he told me that he'd written a poem in Tania's memory. Then, as we filmed, he read it, out loud. It was the most beautiful of moments, as he paid tribute to his "loving, sensitive girl who never hurt anyone."

The wider community found many ways to pay its respects. A candlelit church service was held at Copdock, to try to provide some comfort for those who knew the victims, not that far away from the spot where two of the bodies were found. There was a minute's silence

101

before Ipswich Town's match against Leeds United at Portman Road. The ground sat at the very heart of the red-light district.

So far, this case had seen us shuttling between locations but, on Tuesday, 19ᵗʰ December, the focus settled squarely on just one - London Road in Ipswich, where, at around 5am in the morning, police made an arrest. It took a couple of hours for news of the activity on the ground to filter out, but I eventually got the call and headed down. When I arrived at the junction of London Road and Elliott Street, the police seemed everywhere. A few people were also milling around, claiming to know everything, but actually unable to offer anything remotely reliable. Indeed, the day would provide a salient reminder of the need to take care. Some reporters had already been given the name of the person one local believed they'd seen being led away and, given the pressure everyone felt to be first in breaking the news, it was thankful that no one did, as the person named wasn't involved at all. The man they had arrested at his home, on suspicion of murdering all five women, was actually fork-lift driver Steve Wright. He was 48 at the time. Outwardly a quiet, unassuming man; secretly, a jury would later conclude, a cold-blooded killer.

Wright's home was protected by an extensive cordon. We were keen to get closer, if we could, to gather some shots of the house and, knowing the layout of the neighbourhood, we managed to skirt our way round to the back of the properties on the opposite side of the road and, specifically, a property being used for bed and breakfast. Its owner graciously agreed to let us go through and up the stairs to the front bedroom, which overlooked directly Wright's front door. We'd only been there a few minutes when the sound of footsteps, clumping their way up the stairs behind us, warned of the arrival of other reporters and photographers, who'd had the same idea and also been allowed to take advantage of what was clearly a key vantage-point. Confident that we had everything we needed, we slid away, and the next in line slid in.

Back at police headquarters at Martlesham, the area in front of the building now resembled some kind of camping area. There was a string of gazebos and canopies erected by the main entrance, to provide a sheltered live spot for presenters from all the networks - BBC, ITV,

Channel 4, Five News, plus others - while the car park was filled with outside-broadcast vehicles, mobile homes with awnings, and countless crew and reporter cars.

And, two days after the arrest, we were back in the hall, standing ready for a packed news conference, as Stewart Gull confirmed that Wright had been charged with all five killings. Michael Crimp, from the Crown Prosecution Service, sat beside him and told reporters that they had been working with officers for eight days and had now decided that there was sufficient evidence to authorise that the defendant should be charged. But, in doing so, he warned the media to take care in the way they reported the case, adding, "Stephen Wright stands accused of these offences and has the right of a fair trial before a jury. It is extremely important that this should be responsible media reporting, which should not prejudice the due process of law." Wright appeared before magistrates in Ipswich the following day.

The trial itself started at Ipswich Crown Court just over a year later, on Monday, 14th January 2008. As you'd expect, the media interest was immense, not just from around the country, but from around the world. Within the BBC, we'd been discussing how we'd organise coverage for weeks, to ensure that all the various outlets within the Corporation could get the access and material they wanted. Sky News built a temporary studio, perched on the top of a building just down the road from the court.

There was, for all of us, a huge sense of anticipation as we made our way inside, through security. All of us keen to see the defendant himself in court, in the flesh. I had covered many cases involving people accused of murder, and it's an odd thing to look across the court, into the eyes of an alleged killer. I always found myself trying to step inside their mind, to try to understand how this moment felt. Were they completely detached from what was happening, or did they understand completely the scale of this moment, always hoping that a "not guilty" verdict would come, but fearing more the inevitability of confinement, for a minimum of 15 years? Essential belongings in a bag. Prison van waiting in the courtyard. On the edge of the precipice.

Given the huge media presence, only a limited number of reporters were allowed access into the main court, while the remainder watched and listened to the proceedings from another room. So, this was it. Regina v Steve Gerald James Wright; but there would be no damning piece of evidence. No one saw the killings take place. No murder weapon. No certainty, either, how three of the victims had died. This case would rely on CCTV footage in the red-light area; on DNA from the defendant found on some of the bodies, along with fibres from his car and home; on evidence from neighbours who heard banging.

As one of my BBC colleagues described it so eloquently at the time, the case against Wright "had to be painted in subtle shades, rather than primary colours." In the words of the prosecution barrister, Peter Wright QC, "As to what drives a man to embark upon a campaign such as this we may never know, but, in late October 2006, something caused Wright to engage in such a campaign."

The defendant had replied consistently, "No comment", during police interviews after his arrest, and in court, too, he was a man of few words. He claimed the evidence against him was pure coincidence. Under cross-examination, he would rely on a repetitive series of answers. "It would seem so, yes." "It would appear so, yes," or "If you say so, yes."

For all of us waiting eagerly on the press benches for a key line which might help us understand and portray what he'd been thinking and feeling, there was only a sense of disappointment. The most animated response came when the prosecutor challenged him, "The fact is, there are no coincidences in this case, are there, Mr Wright? The fact is that you murdered each of these women." "No, I did not," he insisted.

In terms of coverage, our chief reporter, Kim Riley, and I worked closely together. Invariably, Kim would be in the main court and would step outside, often with minutes to spare, to provide a live report into the Look East lunchtime bulletin, while I would be in the adjoining court, and could then slip out and disappear to whatever location the evidence of that day's session demanded, to film areas of interest and record a piece to camera to try to put some of the facts squarely in context. We were also well-served by the Crown Prosecution Service, who gave us quick and easy access to the CCTV footage, maps, pictures of cars, clothing and other exhibits which had been shown to the jury, which were essential in helping enhance the story we told to the audience every day.

Continuity, for both Kim and I, was key, ensuring that we understood all the nuances in the case, the significance of key parts of the evidence, and could build things up layer by layer as the facts emerged and the story unfolded. And, as mentioned before, the key thing in all of this was hitting the right tone. It never escaped any of us - not for a single moment - that we were dealing with a case involving the utmost tragedy. The faces of the family and friends of the victims were a constant reminder of the pain and heartache.

The trial lasted six weeks and, as with all cases, but especially with this one, the days when you're waiting for a verdict to come, once the jury has been sent out of the courtroom to reach a decision, are always edgy. At a moment's notice, everyone can suddenly be called back into court, although a helpful word, or a knowing shake of the head from one of the key players, would normally reassure you that it's probably no more than a question from the jury for the judge to try to answer.

But eventually, for Wright, judgement day was upon us. A court can always seem to take an age to reassemble, and the wait this time, as the large number of people involved filed slowly back in, seemed to go on and on but, finally, the verdicts were on their way. This was the only time, in some 40-odd years of court reporting, that my hand was shaking, as I waited, notebook ready, pen poised to jot down every word in shorthand. Then they came, quickly, one after the other. The jury foreman was asked, on each count, if they'd reached verdicts on which they'd all agreed. Yes, was the answer. All five verdicts, all guilty, all unanimous. It had taken them eight hours of deliberation in all. Wright showed no emotion, staring straight ahead. The judge, Mr Justice Gross, thanked the jury and said he'd pass sentence first thing the following day. I sped from court, only to be hit by a sense of panic as I emerged outside onto the court steps. No sign of a camera crew. The alarm soon subsided. To my relief, bursting with a story to tell, they were round the corner and quickly on the scene. I can only imagine, in hindsight, that the verdicts had come a little faster than some had expected, but perhaps those few minutes standing and waiting were a good thing, giving me precious time to compose my thoughts before recording a piece to camera, to sum up all the emotion of the historic moment we'd just witnessed.

Passing sentence 24 hours later, the judge said Wright should never be released and should serve a whole-life term for the killings. This was, he told him, "A targeted campaign of murder. It is right you should spend your whole life in prison." Again, from the defendant, no emotion.

That night, Look East broadcast live from the atrium at Endeavour House, the council building just across the road from the court, and within walking distance of the town's red-light area. It was the most powerful of programmes, as we sought to describe, in 26-odd minutes, the utterly indescribable. As well as telling the story of the day, and of the past year or more, I had been asked by the producer to return towards the end of the programme to offer a summary of my thoughts. How do you distil all that down into some 45 seconds? I thought about the day by the fishery at Hintlesham, after the first body was found; of Jim Duell's poem for Tania; of how that sense of pre-Christmas joy on the streets of Ipswich had been replaced by one of absolute fear; of the church vigil at Copdock, with pictures of the victims placed beside candles of remembrance burning; of the haunting sound of nothing else but the hooves of horses carrying a coffin towards the church at Rushmere St Andrew for the funeral of one of the victims; and, most of all, the words of the judge and that line saying that these women didn't deserve to die, and they certainly didn't deserve to die like this. As I reached that final bit, I could feel the emotion building inside of me. It was only afterwards that my editor told me that, for a moment, she thought I was about to cry. I don't think she knew how true that was. How could you not feel so utterly moved, being so close for so long to something so utterly tragic?

Chapter Sixteen

Getting Noticed!

In one of the earlier chapters, I touched upon the odd business of getting recognised and it felt worthy of further exploration, giving the telling title of this book.

I think it was the delightful Stephen Fry who spoke about people's desire to "touch the cloak of celebrity."

I myself was partial to it from an early age. Always the first one to spot a famous face, and I can well remember being overcome with excitement as a teenage Sea Scout, when I found out that the TV presenter who fronted the local ITV news would be opening our modest little fete in Ipswich. There was something special about seeing someone off the small screen in the flesh.

But then the tables were turned and, of course, it would be disingenuous of me to try to insist that I never savoured the idea of getting noticed, although, as the American writer Diablo Cody noted, "To enjoy being famous, you need to have a screw loose!"

It is, of course, as I've mentioned before, a positive help if people know the face when you turn up unannounced on their doorstep. Trust already established, what do you need to know?

But it does take time to adjust to the fact that there is no demarcation. If you're popping into people's front rooms every night, they have a right to believe that they know you like a friend of the family. So, it really should've been no surprise to me that, when I was standing having a wee in a public toilet, the guy next to me wanted to talk about Look East. "What's the story today then, mate? Anything exciting?!"

He kept his eyes fixed firmly on mine, thankfully, desperate to know more, even following me as I zipped up my trousers and headed for the wash basins, adding, "W'as that Stewart White really like, then?!"

It hardly seemed the right moment, but then it hardly seemed fair for me to be anything other than friendly and polite.

While in the supermarket, someone sidled up to ask," Ooh, what are you doing in here, then?" I really felt they expected more than just, "Er, my shopping". Again, came the expectant "Bit of scandal going on, is there?" Er, no.

The reality, of course, is that you're never off duty, and I'm convinced that you very quickly - even with a very minimal exposure to the limelight - develop a split personality. Are they talking to me as Kevin Burch off the telly; or Kevin Burch as just plain old me? Even without realising it, you start to put on a front, a performance; you start being on your guard. You become used to getting clocked and people doing that second take, or whispering to each other in your wake.

My wife, Sally, always noticed it far more than I did and, even when we got married and headed to the delightful town of Ilkley, in West Yorkshire, for our honeymoon, there was no escape.

In our hotel, the staff always laid out the same table for us in a corner, with the unmistakable strains of the American-Brazilian singer, Bebel Gilberto, creating the most romantic atmosphere.

But, on the first night at dinner, we both became aware of one woman who just kept staring our way. Every time we looked up, she was still there - transfixed on our every move.

The next night - same again. I thought perhaps she'd worked out that we were a honeymoon couple and was utterly fascinated by our body language, not that it struck us as particularly lovey-dovey. It was only when I gazed out of the restaurant window to see a coach parked outside and, on the back, the name of the company, based in Great Yarmouth, the Look East heartland. So, no surprise when the woman in question eventually plucked up the courage to wander across to our table and ask the inevitable, "Aren't you the bloke off the telly?!" Mystery solved.

Some people, though, couldn't be convinced. Once, at a party in a village hall, a guy approached because he knew the friends that we were with, to ask me, "I know you from somewhere, don't I?"

I told him it was probably through the BBC, as I appeared on the telly with Look East.

"No", he insisted, "It's not that. Don't tell me! I'll get it."

We exchanged glances around the table until, finally, he hit that Eureka moment. "I know. You work for John Grose, the car dealers!"

Despite my denials, he wouldn't be told. It might've been easier if I'd conceded defeat earlier and started extolling the features of the new Ford Focus, but he walked away still confused. At least it gave us all a giggle.

Once, at a wedding, a guest stumbled over to ask if she could have a picture taken with me. I wasn't really in the mood, given that we were having the perfect night with old friends, but I agreed, so she grabbed my hand and yanked me off into another room and towards a guy who was scowling with a face like thunder. "Look who it is," she announced proudly, "We're gonna get a picture." To which her partner replied, "I'm not having my picture taken with him!" What's a man to do? "Look, really," I explained, "It's not a problem," but, as I tried to head back to my table, she became even more insistent. The picture was taken and, once calm had been restored, the guy explained that, because of his job, it wouldn't look good having his picture taken with someone involved with the media. I understood totally, but how embarrassing?

That was always the worst scenario, when someone who was a big fan of the programme would say in front of others, "You know who this is, don't you?!" to which the clear answer was obviously, no, not a clue. "He's on the telly." "Never watch the telly, it's shite." Climb gracefully out of that one!

And so many people often got plain confused about who you were. In fact, it became something of a standing joke between my dear Look East colleague, Mike Liggins, and me, given the number of times he would be mistaken for me and vice versa.

One of the funniest moments happened on the seafront at Lowestoft, during the annual air show. Les was on the camera, and we'd just delivered a live piece into the lunchtime bulletin from the beach. As we walked back, a lady asked, "Excuse me, could I have a picture taken with you?" I was always flattered that people took the trouble to ask, so, of course, I said yes. She then turned to her partner and said - quite loudly - "Quick, get the camera, I'm going to have my picture taken with Mike Liggins!"

And there's the dilemma. Do I correct her and tell her that it's actually me, or do I carry on regardless? Of course, I opted for the easy option and didn't even bat an eyelid when she said, after taking the snap, "Thanks, Mike - you're my favourite!"

Never a good thing to get ideas above your station, because moments like that will always remind you that, while you've made your mark, it's probably not quite as clear-cut as you think it is.

Make the slightest error on screen and, again, woe betide you. I once mixed up the words "may" and "might" in a sentence. To quote a footballing phrase, one viewer went in totally two-footed, telling me that I should be ashamed of the fact that I clearly hadn't had a proper education and should instantly have known the different meaning of the two.

The only defence, I always believed at moments like this, was two hands in the air, and say sorry. The fact that he couldn't for one moment have understood the intense pressure under which we were working 24-7 was immaterial. He was right and I was wrong, and that's what it's like working for the BBC. It aspires to be the best of the best, so we had the highest standards to maintain and there was no half-way house. It had to be spot-on and accurate, no matter what.

But, by and large, I've enjoyed nothing but positive feedback and support from the audience, for which I always was, and will be, eternally grateful. People bringing you a hot drink on cold days, offering you a warm room or wi-fi inside their home and, when I finally hung up the metaphorical camera and laptop, so many comments came in about my work which genuinely left me speechless - for once. None of us truly knows the impact of what we do has on ordinary people, until the fat lady sings. Even now, random people tell you how much they miss you. One drinker in a pub who, at the time, it has to be stressed, was totally sober, wandered over as Sally and I were enjoying a quiet drink, to say a heartfelt thank-you for everything I'd done. It was always, it has to be said, my pleasure. Reflecting on that careers book I picked up all those years ago, asking if you fancied a life in news; yes I did, and it didn't disappoint, not for a single second.

Another lay-by - another late edit. Barton Mills. Picture: John Fairhall

Chapter Seventeen

The Future

I started writing this book about the same time that I finally decided that it was the right moment to leave the BBC after some 30 years, the bulk of that working as Suffolk Reporter for BBC Look East. To say I feel blessed to have been given that opportunity is a huge understatement. I'm Ipswich born and bred, and I just love this county. It's so rich in natural beauty, big skies, and wonderfully varied landscapes. I can remember, when I worked in radio, delighting in a trail we thought up to promote Suffolk and it went something like, "From the Newmarket Gallops to the Heritage Coast - from the Waveney Valley to Constable Country, this is BBC Radio Suffolk!" That says it all. Rich in history, too; just recently, we've seen the release of *The Dig* on Netflix, telling the story of the humble heroics in 1939 of Suffolk's very own Basil Brown and the discovery of the Anglo-Saxon ship burial at Sutton Hoo. Treasure beyond words … beyond value. Who could not be utterly captivated by what happened in our own back yard? And the people. So kind, so generous - invariably, once you get to know them - and prepared to open up their lives and their hearts and trust you. Yes, trust. That matters more than anything. To be trusted in a business which, if one recent survey is to be relied upon (CV-Library 2019), comes second in a league table of who's trusted least in the UK. Politicians were top!

I couldn't honestly bang the drum for a chunky percentage of the people working in this industry, but I will vouch ferociously for the integrity of a fair few. People who work tirelessly, passionately to dig out and share the story. Often in the face of huge danger or just downright unsavoury and unjustifiable criticism, from people who don't know what the job entails - keyboard warriors, comfy at home - or don't care

Christchurch Park, Ipswich. 2020. Picture: John Fairhall

to find out, yet still yell "Fake News" and seek to undermine the huge importance of the Fourth Estate. It is pernicious and a precarious place to be, not just for the honest and hard-working reporters and camera crews, but for anyone who truly believes in democracy, accountability, speaking truth to power. The BBC gets it wrong sometimes, of course it does, but, from what I've seen during my stint, it's always been a cock-up, not a conspiracy. Like I said at the beginning, I've never been asked to skew a story, to put a slant on the facts. It's never happened. Never would on my watch. What would be the point of that? Naïve maybe, but I like it that way.

So now it's freelancing. A new chapter, a new challenge, as we launch our own business - Burchmedia. Original, eh?! Looking to slow the speed of the roundabout just a little, while retaining the best bits - the film-making, the editing, alongside new areas such as media-training and podcast production - and holding tightly onto by far the most important thing of all, and that's getting the chance still to work with fascinating and funny people - the positive, the kind and the generous.

But looking back, boy, it's been a hoot. From scones to scoops, it always felt like the right call, and I can do no more now than offer my heartfelt thanks to everyone who's helped me along the way and feel grateful beyond words for the chances that I've been given. Let's see where the road winds now. On we go. Onwards and upwards.

Cheers! Suffolk Show 2017

About the author

Kevin Burch is an award-winning journalist, who lives in Suffolk and has savoured a long career in the media, working in local newspapers and BBC local radio, at BBC Television Centre in London and then, for more than twenty years, as a TV reporter and presenter with BBC Look East. He now runs his own media business and is also a passionate Ipswich Town fan and wildlife volunteer.

This book follows his journalistic journey, from college and cub reporter, to covering one of Britain's biggest crime stories, from funny moments to famous faces. It's dedicated to his family and friends, and all the media colleagues, who've either helped make him what he is, or simply made him giggle. You know who you are!

Weren't you that bloke off the telly?

Thumbs-up! Messing about on the water with Stephen Huntley

Three men in a beach hut at Felixstowe. Picture: John Fairhall

116

Weren't you that bloke off the telly?

Young reporter, up church tower, looking lost. Picture: EADT

Fast food, slow pace with Jamie Niblock

Weren't you that bloke off the telly?

A stunning place: Ramsholt in 2017

Sailing in Blue Goose with John Fairhall and Richard Daniel

118

Another day at court, another deadline

Chips with everything. Picture: John Fairhall

The power of Pudsey!

The Ferryman: Taken during a blissful day's filming at Butley Ferry